More Than You Can Handle

Life is Full of the Overwhelmingly Unexpected

by

Doug Moore, M.D.

DO MOORE PUBLISHING
BIRMINGHAM, AL

Doug Moore, MD
2520 Valleydale Road
Birmingham, Al 35244

More Than You Can Handle: Life is Full of the Overwhelmingly Unexpected/
ISBN 978-0692933435

1. Christian 2. Inspirational 3. Personal Growth 4. Self-Help
1st Edition

Illustrations and Cover design: Susan E. Meyer
Book Production and Editor: jamesgang creative

On the web at: MoreThanYouCanHandle.com

PREFACE v

Chapter One - The "Verse" 3

    Fiction or Misquote 4

    God's Part in the Battles 7

    Gideon's Example 10

    A Holy Trend 10

    The Source of Grandma's Verse 11

Chapter Two - Ask More Questions 15

    Everything. 16

    Jesus' Example 18

    No "Cookie Cutter" Formula 19

    Abiding 21

    Pause.. 22

    Examine Your Motives 23

    Ask 23

Chapter Three - Bad Things 27

    First, let's define "bad." 29

    The Contract 31

    "It Was Good" 34

    Judge Correctly... 36

    Event Reality.. 37

    Job's View 39

Chapter Four - God Expectations 42

    Unexpected Outcomes.................................... 45

    The Three "D's" of God-Directed Discomfort.... 47

    Dog Nights... 49

Chapter Five - "BTABS" 54

    BTABS Origin 56

    Skateboard Dilemmas 57

    Nurturing the Nature 60

Chapter Six - Muddy Water **64**

The Three-Legged Stool... 66

Spirit Priority... 69

Worldly Misleadings.. 70

Chapter Seven - Dam Fixing **74**

Leaking Dam Reality 76

Healthy Spirit 77

Spiritual Diagnosis/Treatment 78

The Enemy.. 79

Chapter Eight - Body and Soul................................... **84**

Body.. 85

Using Medicine... 87

Soul Treatment... 90

Chapter Nine - Facing the Unexpected...................... **95**

Life Battles With Others... 96

Jesus Failed 99

An Improved Word Picture 101

Chapter Ten - Soaring in the Storm **106**

Answered Prayer.. 108

Compromised Days in God's Hands...........................111

Paul's View... 112

The Redeeming of the Permanent............................ 113

Soaring Free: Verses That Will Mean More 114

Epilogue... **121**

A Goal and a Contrast.. 121

Contrasting Stories 123

The Eagle Will Land 128

About the Author **129**

PREFACE

Until I was in my mid 20's, I was moderately clueless as to how hard life can be. I'm not sure why I was so clueless. Maybe I'm a slow learner. Maybe my parents provided a blindly secure upbringing. Maybe I hid from life's battles; Well, other than battling my three brothers! But, Med school and the world of medicine teach more than anatomy and physiology. Away from the backwoods of my Alabama farm, I found life to be more complicated and hard.

As a family practice physician, one of the most important things I need to know is to know what I don't know. I have to be able to see a situation and realize I don't have the knowledge base to address what's going on. The next thing I need to possess is the willingness to admit what I don't know and deal with it; deal with it by either getting someone who does know or become educated regarding the issue that befuddles me.

One thing I do know, I haven't got it all together. As my pastor says, "We all got issues." And, "all" includes me. I'm not as messed up, ignorant, hardheaded, angry, bitter, cowardly, selfish, etc. as I once was. Years (and I mean years) of study and hundreds of self-help books and hundreds of hours of being mentored by others and several times reading through the Bible, have corrected many of my issues.

2 Corinthians 1:3-7 shares that the struggles of our lives become useful to God in helping others with the same struggles. One fruit of my struggles is *More Than You Can Handle*. When I look in the rear view mirror of my life, and ponder some of my

struggles, I have come to one common theme: Too often I and those around me were merely treating the symptoms of our issues and not recognizing the root issues.

The reasons for this are numerous. Sometimes the symptoms were very serious and needed to be dealt with. Often we were ill-equipped to recognize that they were symptoms. We were deceived. We were very good at fooling ourselves. We also failed to consider the full impact that we have an Enemy whose goal is to steal, kill and destroy. That Enemy is well equipped to bring half-truth. We are just as good at believing half-truths. We are too busy, prideful, tired, distorted, lazy ... to pick up the Bible and follow the examples of the Bereans (Acts 17:11) who examined the Scriptures every day to see if what they were being told was true when compared to Scripture.

My own life struggles led me to some great mentors and Biblical insights. In my office, I've seen patients experiencing the same miseries as I had survived. Sharing struggles with these patients became a common occurrence in my practice. The solutions discovered led me to organize those lessons into printed form. My goal is to help those who have lost hope when they feel overwhelmed. My hope is that God gets glory as this material moves people closer to Him as they fight the battles found in this hard life. This book doesn't have all the answers to life's struggles. I pray it helps its readers ask The One who is the Answer.

- Doug Moore

DEDICATION

God has been good to me. All glory and honor and praise related to my life goes to Him.

I thank my beautiful wife for her steadfast commitment to me as she endured the development of this material.

This book is dedicated to Dave Lewis, a genuine man who held my feet firmly in the Word of God during the great storm of my life.

ACKNOWLEDGEMENTS

Thanks to my mom and dad who first put me on the foundation of God's truths.

To my book screeners (Jim, Gary, KC, Carol, Mike C., Leslie, Bobby, Todd, Brian, Andy, Jason, Tom, Mike B., Zac, Dave, Audrey, Wilson, Austin, and Chandler), Thanks! A very extra special thanks to Jim Kelly and Gary Ohmstede for the multiple extra miles in helping me fine tune, organize, and express what was in my head.

Thanks to my teachers/mentors: Steve Holloway, John Riddle, Frank Barker, Bob Stone, Chris Hodges and Harry Reeder.

Thanks to Church of the Highlands for providing me with the encouragement and support to take my next steps. Thanks to my editor, Gary James, who is a wonderful clean up artist.

Lastly, this book's development is forever joined with the legacy left by **Ashlynn Bailey, Drake Holder, Bailey McAvoy, Elle Campbell, Collier Ann Byers, and Madison McManus** whose very short lives continue to strengthen the hope of those left behind in the wake of the overwhelming unexpected.

More Than
You
Can Handle

CHAPTER ONE

The "Verse"

"The Lord isn't going to put any more on you
than you can handle."
- Someone's Grandmother

Life is hard.

The story unfolded like a made-for-TV movie. It wasn't long after the car wreck in which her sister died that she was told her mother had breast cancer. Then came her son's alcohol use causing him to be expelled from school. Her husband's job had turned south with the economy. Their church's internal leadership conflict led to the loss of several friends. Her best friend moved away to Colorado to be near her kids. Strange as it sounds, the final straw was the death of an old faithful pet. Tired and sleepless nights led her to come for help. In my office, she sat with a painted face and a plastic smile.

The chart read, "Chief complaint: fatigue." Further questioning revealed a pattern of appetite changes, poor sleep, withdrawal from society and irritability. Her physical exam was unremarkable except for her being too short for the weight she carried. I refer to this as "height-challenged" because it seems to sound better than saying overweight. Blood tests showed no abnormalities. I pondered the possible medical diagnoses: Grief ... Depression ... Adjustment disorder with depressed mood ... Anemia ... Low thyroid ... then I asked, "How are you handling all this?"

There's a reason doctors keep tissues at the bedside. It's the same reason ambulances are at football games. The same reason water is at the end of marathons or mops are kept in school cafeterias. Each will be needed at some point.

When I asked the question, the inevitable tears exploded. It was as if she had been storing up a lake of them. She had protected herself from this moment so many times. Yet, the vulnerability of the doctor's office and the promise of secrecy the physician patient relationship entails demanded the tearing down of walls. After about eight tissues, she gathered enough composure to confess the obvious, "I'm not handling it well at all." Then she puzzled, "But I know the Bible says, 'The Lord isn't going to put any more on you than you can handle.'"

There it was again, the "Verse." For over two decades now, I've been searching Scripture for it. Patients have quoted it to me more than any Bible verse.

Fiction or Misquote

It's a fallen world, a cursed world. Pain, accidents, illness, death and disappointments occur daily. Even Hollywood knows this. I recently read a quote from John Wayne, "Life is tough. It's even tougher if you're stupid."

As Christians, we are not promised a life of bliss. There is an abundance of prosperity teaching in the world. Yet, throughout the Bible we find the opposite is often seen. King David, a man "after God's own heart," had a family racked with discord and violence. Moses' leadership was repeatedly challenged. Elijah ran in fear. Paul was stoned and imprisoned. Jesus was

4

ridiculed, misunderstood and misrepresented by the religious leaders of his day.

Scripture would indicate that life being smooth and easy is not guaranteed on this side of heaven. Each of us can recall upstanding Christian men and women who have experienced significant hardship and trials that were overwhelming. The testimony of life speaks of times of struggles.

Into all this comes the oft repeated "verse," i.e. "The Lord isn't going to put more on you than you can handle." I refer to this as "Grandma's Verse" because it so often seems that an encouraging and thoughtful grandmother-like figure has been placed in each of our lives. It is from that grandmother-like person that we have so often heard these words meant to encourage and empower us.

The problem is, there is no such Bible verse. It's not there. Go ahead. Put this book down, grab your Bible and try to find it. Go ahead. Use your concordance, your computer, your Pastor. You won't find it. You'll get close only once. You will laugh at me and say, "I found it!!!! There it is: 1 Corinthians 10:13."

However, look closer at the verse:

> "No temptation has seized you except what is common to man. And, God is faithful; he will not let you be tempted beyond what you can bear. But when you are tempted, he will also provide a way out so that you can stand up under it" (1 Corinthians 10:13)

This verse speaks of temptation. Here Paul is only dealing with those moments in our lives when we are faced with an opportunity to live outside of God's will. In Grandma's Verse, God is the author of a situation in which we have the capacity within ourselves to handle. In Corinthians, God is our guide to escape from temptations.

Let me demonstrate: You're watching TV and the nature of the show becomes such that the Holy Spirit within you lets you know that you shouldn't be watching any longer. Yet, you're tempted to continue to watch. There is a way of escape. You can hit the "off" button ... leave the room ... throw a brick though the TV.

How about this scenario: You're walking down the street when the man in front of you pulls his hand out of his pocket and out falls a $100 bill. He is clueless and continues to walk on. You're tempted. The electric bill was higher for you this month ... your kid's school play costume needs to be paid for ... the missionary who spoke last week at church needs financial support ... In each situation, you have prayed and asked God to provide. And low and behold, here's a $100 "donation"!!! You are tempted. Yet, again, there is a way of escape from the temptation ... call to the man and let him know of his mistake.

Grandma's Verse isn't 1 Corinthians 10:13. Grandma's Verse is possibly a perversion of Paul's words. It's a return of the Enemy's common ploy: employ half-truths. He knows, half-truths are often more powerful than full lies. It's a ploy he first used against Adam and Eve (Genesis 3). He tried it with Jesus in the desert temptation scene (Matthew 4). Satan for sure could be behind this perversion. In addition, our own sinful nature would contribute to this perversion, also. Our bent is to do things without God and even against God, to do things on our own. To say, "I got this."

Grandma's Verse tries to eliminate God as being a part of bringing us into the battles we are up against. In effect, it says, "God wouldn't do this to you!" Bible stories reveal this view is not true.

God's Part in the Battles

What part is God playing in Grandma's Verse? It could be saying, "He didn't bring this on you. It came from somewhere else." On the other hand, it could be, "He has gifted you with the means/gifts/talents to bring about an easy resolution to the current situation." How do these options line up with characters and stories from the Bible?

Let's first look at Moses. Here the great leader is in Egypt leading the Jewish nation to freedom. He knows to lean on God. After all, God is the one who sent the Plagues and set up Israel's escape from slavery. So where is Moses sent by God on this escape route? God directs the escape route to be down a road that leads to a dead end at a seashore. One side of the proverbial "rock and a hard place" has been set.

Then we find God working in a way that most of us find uncomfortable to contemplate as He orchestrates the remaining side of the "rock and hard place." In Exodus 7:3-4 God is speaking and describing what he is about to do to the man who has the keys to the Israelite's freedom.

> "But I will harden Pharaoh's heart, and though
> I multiply my miraculous signs and wonders in
> Egypt, he will not listen to you" (Exodus 7:3-4)

This action of God is seen several times in subsequent chapters of the Exodus story. God describes his "hardening" of Pharaoh's heart. The final "hardening" is found in Exodus 14:8.

> "The Lord hardened the heart of Pharaoh king of Egypt, so that he pursued the Israelites, who were marching out boldly" (Exodus 14:8)

My momma raised me to be nice to people. She and the folks in my Ol' rural Alabama community would frown on any behavior that put anybody in dire straights. She taught me a lot about God. These verses didn't seem to show the same God I had been introduced to in my upbringing. Yet, here they are. Then a wise man showed me what these verses represent. They are using a word picture to describe a sovereign aspect of God.

All goodness that exists in anybody comes from God. Essentially, the goodness in a person is "on loan" from God. (Yeah, Rush Limbaugh may be partially right here). God is under no obligation to maintain that "loaned" goodness. He can, and does, at his choosing, recall some of that "loaned" goodness.

The word picture here in relation to Pharaoh is that of a mud puddle. The puddle begins as a mixture of water and dirt. The sun shining on a mud puddle will cause the water to be evaporated. The water is withdrawn from the puddle. In so doing, the mud begins a process of hardening. God's "hardening" of Pharaoh's heart is that of God recalling some of His goodness that He had loaned Pharaoh. The word picture in the Exodus hardening verses is that God's goodness is the water; Pharaoh's sinful nature is the dirt.

God was leaving Pharaoh to make decisions based on Pharaoh's own sinful choice. God, being omniscient, all knowing, knew what Pharaoh would do. Pharaoh would change his mind and pursue Moses and the people of Israel. The other half of the "rock and the hard place" was now in place: Orchestrated by God.

See the scene and notice: God placed them there at that time and place, in way over their heads. Over a million people trapped between a sea and an army of death. Did they say that the God-directed situation they were in was more than they could handle? Yes! Look at Exodus 14:10-12 and see their response to the situation:

> "As Pharaoh approached, the Israelites looked up, and there were the Egyptians, marching after them. They were terrified and cried out to the Lord. They said to Moses, 'was it because there were no graves in Egypt that you brought us to the desert to die? What have you done to us by bringing us out of Egypt? Didn't we say to you in Egypt, leave us alone; let us serve the Egyptians? It would have been better for us to serve the Egyptians than to die in the desert!'" (Exodus 14:10-12)

They evaluated their situation and essentially said, "We're gonna die! There is no way anyone can handle this!" Yet, that's not what Moses saw. He agreed that it was more than they could handle. But, he also saw God behind the scene working deliverance. There was no quoting Grandma's Verse by Moses.

Gideon's Example

An even clearer example of Grandma's Verse not being Biblical is found in the story of Gideon told in the book of Judges. Judges 6-7 finds the nation of Israel in an impending battle with the Midianite army. Gideon had an army of 30,000 men to fight the 135,000-man Midianite army. Not exactly good odds for our hero! God was aware of this situation and addressed it. Here is the short version of God's response:

"You have too many men ..." (Judges 6:2)

God wanted fewer men! He even gives His reasoning: "In order that Israel may not boast against me that her own strength has saved her ..."

What a staggering statement in light of the witness of those who say God doesn't let us be overwhelmed. God instructs Gideon to implement a plan to reduce his odds of winning. God wants the situation to be humanly insurmountable. In the end, Gideon's army is reduced to 300 men. Three hundred men to go against at least 135,000! Only then was God satisfied with the circumstances facing Gideon. God chose this position for Gideon. There is no "God isn't going to give you more than you can handle" mentality found here. It *was* more than Gideon could handle.

A Holy Trend

Examine the other Biblical adventures: David and Goliath (1 Samuel 17); Joshua up against Jericho (Joshua 6); Shadrach, Meshach and Abednego in the fiery furnace (Daniel 3); Elijah at

Mt. Carmel (1 Kings 18); Mary's unwed pregnancy (Matthew 1, Luke 1); Samson and the "jaw bone" battle (Judges 15).

The Source of Grandma's Verse

What is the origin of Grandma's Verse? The prior discussion would disallow God or His Word as the source. There would only be two remaining possibilities: Man and/or Satan.

In Genesis, the story of Eve and the serpent interactions is revealed. Eve is told that she's not quite God, yet that it is within her capabilities to become as God. She is encouraged to take the fruit and eat. She and Adam can handle it. They do eat it. They can't handle it.

Man has since refined the variations of our being able, with God's gifts, to handle the dilemmas of our lives. Adam hid to handle his problem. Cain killed to handle his issues. Abraham got a second wife. Elijah ran. The Pharisees followed rules. Peter betrayed. Pilate abdicated his responsibilities.

My "being able to handle it," ultimately reflects a theology of me not needing God and second-guessing His plan. A view that leads to taking God's gifts and abilities and putting them in place of God. It reflects a theology where my talents and resources are all that are needed to conquer my adversaries. It reveals the idea that God gave me the tools, and then He has stepped back to watch. This theology isn't found in Moses, Gideon, David, Elijah or any other man after God's own heart. With them and others of their bent, we find people who use God-given talents and abilities while totally depending on Him.

The ultimate example of our being unable to "handle it" lies in our sin. As sinful, unforgiven creatures, we are spiritually dead. We are incapable of purifying ourselves in the eyes of a Holy God. We cannot "work off" our sins. Spiritually dead people can only do one thing spiritually: be dead. God's plan is for Jesus to pay for our sins. Then we are brought to spiritual life by His grace and mercy leading us to accept that our sin is more than we can handle and we let Him do it all.

Grandma's Verse is a holdover. It echoes Satan's original deception - we can handle it - we can do it on our own. We can't; God can. That's the Gospel. We're in over our heads. There is a source of redemption, but it isn't us. We can't earn it. It's a gift. Jesus saw us unable to handle our sin. He stepped in, paid the price wholly and totally without any contribution from us.

The daily situations that overwhelm us offer an opportunity to handle it or to follow the Biblical examples, instructions, and encouragement. Philippians 4:13 is one of the most encouraging verses:

> "I can do everything through Him who gives me strength" (Philippians 4:13)

This sounds close to Grandma's Verse. However, as we will see in the next chapter, it's not.

Discharge Plan

Self-examination:

- Have you ever spoken "Grandmother's Verse" over a life situation?

- Has anyone spoken "Grandmother's Verse" over your life situation? How did that make you feel?

- What's your impression of the compare/contrast between "Grandmother's Verse" and 1 Corinthians 10:13?

- Have you ever read the Exodus story and wondered about Pharaoh's hard-heart verses?

- Why is it hard to resist taking on life on your own?

- Can you think of a time when you "handled" things on your own terms?

- What current situation are you in that overwhelms you?

Treatment:

- Ask God to help you see where you have left him out of the situation.

- Ask for forgiveness for leaving God out.

Rehab:

"I lift up my eyes to the mountains—where does my help come from? My help comes from the LORD, the Maker of heaven and earth. He will not let your foot slip—he who watches over you will not slumber; indeed, he who watches over Israel will neither slumber nor sleep. The LORD watches over you - the LORD is your shade at your right hand; the sun will not harm you by day, nor the moon by night. The LORD will keep you from all harm—he will watch over your life; the LORD will watch over your coming and going both now and forevermore" (Psalm 121)

"Just Be Held" by Casting Crowns. *Thrive.* Reunion Records. 2014.

CHAPTER TWO

Ask More Questions

"I can do everything through Him who gives me strength" (Philippians 4:13)

Life is hard.

Life is harder if we try to make square pegs fit into round holes. How does a Christian reconcile the concept of being in situations way beyond our control with the scriptures that indicate that we can do everything?

The last year of Family Practice residency comes after several years of studying. To get to that year, an individual has to have gone through four years of undergraduate college studies, four more years of medical school, three years of residency, passed hundreds of tests, passed a Board Medical exam, and endured a lot of one-on-one mentoring by older physicians. I was in that last year with just a few days to go before I began my own medical career when a mentor taught me one of life's most powerful lessons.

While on a hospital learning rotation with two of my fellow residents, we encountered a patient who had a bewildering array of symptoms for which we could find no cause. The three of us were huddled in a room pondering the situation, trying to make sense out of symptoms that made no sense. Our older, wise physician mentor quietly sat and watched us fretting. At that point in our training, it was not appropriate for him to give us the answers. He wouldn't be with us in a few weeks to give answers. His job was to give guiding principles to help when future patients would bewilder us. We talked and pondered and talked and pondered and talked and pondered. Finally, we fell silent realizing we could make no sense of all the data from our mysterious patient.

It was then that the sage mentor spoke. He reviewed how far we had come. He reminded us of how all three of us had endured years of book studies, thousands of hours of direct patient care and been trained by many brilliant specialist. Yet, with all that knowledge the three of us had gleaned we were at a dead end with our current patient. He built us up by stating that we were intellectually prepared to enter the world of medicine. So, why were we about to fail in helping this patient?

Then he spoke wisdom that has gotten me out of many dilemmas in life, not just in medicine. "If it doesn't make sense, you don't have all the facts. Go back and ask more questions."

What was meant by "more questions"? It meant going back to the patient and getting a clearer history of the current illness. It meant asking questions of the people in the patient's life who may have seen things of which the patient was unaware. It meant ordering more labs, x-rays and other studies. Clarify the problem. Define the issues that were critical from those that were just distractions.

Everything.

"I can do all things through Christ who strengthens me" (Philippians 4:13 New King James Version)

Instead of "all things," some other translations use "everything." What is "everything/all things?" Does it mean I am "faster than a speeding bullet, more powerful than a locomotive, able to leap tall buildings in a single bound?" Can I hold my breath for 30 hours? Can I fly to Jupiter? Those don't seem to be what "everything/all things" mean.

Can I fast for a week? Can I resolve conflict at work? Can I write a book (even if my lowest grade in college was in English!!!)? Can I forgive my child's murderer? Can I move from my comfortable community to start a new ministry in a distant town? Those seem closer to the "everything/all things" meaning.

Can I turn water into wine? Can I walk on water? Can I feed five thousand people with my sack lunch? At first glance those seem to be what "everything/all things" meant for one person but not for me.

Can the words I speak be a part of healing cancer? Can I cast out demons? Can I speak to a mountain and have it move to the sea? Those, I am told in scripture, can be part of "everything/all things."

In Jeremiah 32:27, God speaks of Himself: "I am the Lord, the God of all mankind. Is anything too hard for me?" Of course, this is a rhetorical question. God can do anything within His nature. At this point, it would be appropriate to reflect on some of certain characteristics of God.

It is impossible to capture God with ink and paper. Millions of pages have been written chasing that goal. That isn't where this book is headed. Yet, to explore part of His nature will serve as a good foundation for understanding how our overwhelming situations relate to God.

God is, among other things, Omnipotent. That is, He is all-powerful. He can do anything within His nature. (I would suggest you pursue the writings of C.S. Lewis in regards to those odd questions such as "Can God lie?" The answer, of course, is no! That would not be within His nature and therefore if He did lie then He wouldn't be God to begin with.) To be God, He has to be all-powerful and if He is all-powerful, He is God. Nothing is outside His control.

So how are we to reconcile the verses that indicate a believer can do "everything/all things" (as if the believer is Omnipotent) with those verses in which God as able to do anything He desires? Has the unstoppable force met the immovable object? Maybe it's time to "go back and ask more questions."

We have a nature and propensity to want to handle things on our own. That's why we receive Grandma's Verse so readily. It's also the reason that when we read Philippians 4:13 that our focus seems to be on the "I can do all" portion while glossing over the "through Christ" portion. Remember, half-truths are often more dangerous than full lies. We consider the "I can do all" as the focus of the verse when, in reality, "through Christ" is THE point of the verse.

Jesus' Example

Jesus is our example of how to live this "through Him" life. Jesus bluntly told us how he handled life and the issues that came in his life. John 5:19 shows Jesus responding to those who questioned his methods. Read this incredibly revealing verse slowly and a few times over:

"Jesus gave them this answer: 'I tell you the truth, the Son can do nothing by himself; he can do only what he sees his Father doing, because whatever the Father does the Son also does'" (John 5:19)

Jesus boldly proclaims that on his own he "can do nothing." The Holman Christian Standard Bible (HCSB) goes as far as to translate it as, "The Son is not able to do anything on His own ..." Jesus has no knowledge of Grandma's Verse! For Jesus doing "everything/all things" is only found in an ongoing communication and following exactly what the Father had for him to do. John 8:28 reinforces this aspect of Jesus as he informs us that even the words he speaks have been filtered through the Father:

"So Jesus said, 'When you have lifted up the Son of Man, then you will know that I am he and that I do nothing on my own but speak just what the Father has taught me'" (John 8:28)

I like to imagine what that looked and sounded like as Jesus moved through his daily life. It can reveal often-overlooked aspects of God's nature. He doesn't seem to like to be put in a box and He has a sense of humor.

No "Cookie Cutter" Formula

So, taking Jesus at his word, let's walk with him through one aspect of his life. As he moved from place to place and saw opportunities for ministry, his own testimony from John 5 and 8 says he would check off every opportunity with the Father.

19

Biblical evidence would lead one to see the following as a possibility of the Father/Son interaction:

Jesus:
Father, there's a blind man here. Should I heal him?

Father:
Yes.

Jesus:
How? What should I do?

Father:
Speak healing words to him.

Jesus:
Father, there is another blind person. Should I heal him?

Father:
Yes.

Jesus:
How? Should I speak healing words to him?

Father:
No. Touch him.

Jesus:
Father, here's another blind man. Should I heal him?

Father:
Yes.

Jesus:
How? Speak healing words? Touch?

Father:
No. Spit on the ground. Make some spit mud and put it on his eyes.

Jesus:
Oh, that's a good one!! That will mess with people for years!

How wonderful is our God's sense of humor and we often miss it. We also miss the encouragement scripture reveals, without words. We should not put God in the "He did it this way last time, so let's do it like that again" mold. He is no cookie cutter God. Jesus demonstrates that God decides how each situation is handled. We have to "do things through Him."

How then, do we do things through Him? The answer is found by having an abiding relationship with Him.

Abiding

The Bible reveals that once a person has accepted Jesus as their only solution to their spiritually dead state and has Jesus become their savior and Lord, they have an eternal relationship with him. (Romans 8:38-39.) Yet, on this side of heaven, we still have the capabilities to make choices that fall outside of the principles and precepts found in scripture. In those times, we will still have a relationship with God, however our fellowship will be compromised. We will be moving in our own efforts and abilities, essentially embracing Grandma's Verse. That's not the way Jesus did it. It's not the way we should do it.

Jesus in John 15, shares the word picture of his followers being in such a relationship to him as grape branches are to the parent vine. Many have referred to that as an abiding relationship. I'm indebted to John Riddle of Birmingham, AL, for clarifying what this looks like.

21

Abiding involves three distinct parts. There have been many terms used by people. Here I will use the following:

PAUSE

EXAMINE YOUR MOTIVES

ASK

As believers facing the aspects of life, we should move through these and we will find ourselves in that same Jesus/Father Oneness. Most individuals will find using scripture to be a vital tool in this process.

Pause

Sometimes thought of as inviting the Holy Spirit to take over the situation. Others consider it a time of acknowledging who we really are, creatures in over our heads and needing help. It should be a time of thanksgiving and confidence in regards to what God is about to do in the situation. I have found the following verses to be foundational in PAUSE:

"This is the confidence we have in approaching God: that if we ask anything according to his will, he hears us. And if we know that he hears us - whatever we ask - we know that we have what we ask of him" (1 John 5:14-15)

"And he died for all, that those who live should no longer live for themselves but for him who died for them and was raised again" (2 Corinthians 5:15)

22

Examine Your Motives

We are unable not to sin, and often have corrupt motives. This step is where confession of sin and non-Godly promptings occur. It is unrealistic to expect God to have a healthy fellowship with us if we are unwilling to confess our sin. I have found the following verses to be foundational in EXAMINE YOUR MOTIVES:

> "If we confess our sins, he is faithful and just and will forgive us our sins and purify us from all unrighteousness" (1 John 1:9)

> "Search me, O God, and know my heart; test me and know my anxious thoughts. See if there is any offensive way in me, and lead me in the way everlasting" (Psalm 139:23-24)

> "Create in me a pure heart, O God, and renew a steadfast spirit within me" (Psalm 51:10-11)

Ask

This one's pretty straightforward: Ask the Father. The desire here is to be filled with the Holy Spirit in such a way as to have God's wisdom, knowledge, discernment, etc. I have found the following scriptures foundational in ASK:

> "So I say, walk by the Spirit, and you will not gratify the desires of the flesh" (Galatians 5:16)

"If any of you lacks wisdom, you should ask God, who gives generously to all without finding fault, and it will be given to you. But when you ask, you must believe and not doubt, because the one who doubts is like a wave of the sea, blown and tossed by the wind" (James 1:5-6)

These aren't "rubbing the lamp and out pops a genie and get your three wishes granted" steps. They are deeply spiritual. As such, they should be viewed as valuable and worthy of inputting time and energy. The verses suggested with each step have served me well. Other verses can be found to help the person seeking an abiding lifestyle. The vital point is to appropriate verses to use in moving into a position of clear communication/communion with God.

Beginning the process is important. Like most new habits in life, it will seem awkward and mechanical at first. Repetition and subsequent success in battle areas of life will lead to more ease in developing a lifestyle of abiding.

Ask the Father to help you in the process. Ask him to give you some "baby" steps to begin the journey. My first success came in the area of having a heavy foot on the accelerator while driving. I had become aware of how speeding and aggressive driving were not God honoring. I began to PAUSE, EXAMINE MY MOTIVES, and ASK in that area of my life. Soon I found myself being a much more Christ-like driver. It didn't happen overnight. Yet, it did happen. It didn't happen as I expected or in the time I expected. Those expectations were also a battle front that abiding exposed for what they are, useful to the Enemy.

Discharge Plan

Self Examination:

- Have you ever experienced the feeling of inadequacy while reading Philippians 4:13? How did you cope with that?

- Jesus didn't convince everyone he witnessed to or heal the whole world while here on earth. How does that fit with "doing everything?"

- What is your typical "go to" plan when faced with life struggles?

- What is revealed about your fellowship with God in light of where you first go to solve problems?

- What situation are you in now that needs "more questions" ask about?

- What problems arise when we see God as a "He did it this way last time/cookie cutter God?"

- What part of PAUSE, EXAMINE YOUR MOTIVES, ASK do you find the most difficult? What prevents us from Pausing? Examining our motives? Asking?

- How does un-confessed sin present a barrier to pausing?

- Is anything too small to Pause, Examine Your Motives and Ask? If that 's the case, how does that look as we move through our day?

Treatment:

- Ask God to reveal which "baby steps" He desires for you to pursue in developing an abiding life style.

- Memorize or develop a rapid retrieval option (Bible phone app, etc) to have supporting scriptures that can aid the abiding life style brought forth when you PAUSE, EXAMINE YOUR MOTIVES, ASK.

Rehab:

"Remain in me, as I also remain in you. No branch can bear fruit by itself; it must remain in the vine. Neither can you bear fruit unless you remain in me" (John 15:4)

"Place of Freedom" by Highlands Worship. *Place of Freedom*. EMI Christian Music Group. 2012.

CHAPTER THREE

Bad Things

"God saw all that he had made, and it was very good" (Genesis 1:31)

Life is hard.

Life is harder if you take on a job that wasn't yours in the first place.

There's an old Chinese proverb about a man whose wife bore him a baby son. Now, in China, families who have boys were considered especially blessed. When the town's people heard the man had a son they told the new father, "This is good." The father responded, "How do you know this is good?"

As the boy grew, it became apparent to all that he was a mean hellion of a lad. The people of the town spoke of this to the father telling him, "This is bad." The father responded, "How do you know this is bad?"

The mean boy grew into a tough young man. He was mean and tough enough to "break" wild horses. This was a process of riding the wild horse in such a way as to break its will and thus anybody could now ride the horse. Being the only one in the province with such a talent, he soon was making a lucrative living. Now the people returned to the dad and spoke again. "This is good," they declared. The father responded, "How do you know this is good?"

One day the young man met with a horse tougher than he and the young man suffered a broken leg. Since there were no doctors in the town to treat the fracture, it healed improperly and the young man was now crippled. " This is bad," reported the people. The father responded, "How do you know this is bad?"

Soon thereafter an evil Chinese warlord passed through the town and conscripted every able bodied young man for his army. Since these new draftees were mostly farm boys, everyone knew they were to be used as military pawns destined for death. The crippled young man was left in town with his grateful father.

Some chapters in books build to a crescendo of enlightenment at the very end. It's a way of driving home the point. That's not going to be true of this chapter. (Well, sorta.) I will drive the point of this chapter at the end, and here at the beginning, and interspersed within its pages. This chapter's point:

As Christians, we **ARE NOT** given the

Right

Privilege

Honor

Authority

Position

Command

to ever label an event, occurrence, adventure, episode, or hardship as "bad."

Let me make sure that point is driven home. As Christians, we **ARE NOT** given the

Right

Privilege

Honor

Authority

Position

Command

to ever label an event, occurrence, adventure, episode, or hardship as "bad."

Now, take a deep breath: Put the book down and take in that concept.

Okay, now pick up the book again or we won't move forward..

The first thoughts that most of us have when reading the above is that it's not true. It goes against what we "know" to be true. It doesn't make sense that it's not true. Remember, if it doesn't make sense, you may not have all the facts. Ask more questions.

First, let's define "bad"

Here are some of the definitions of "bad" from Webster's dictionary: morally evil, wicked, defective, below standard, worthless, faulty, incorrect, inadequate, not valid, unpleasant, unfavorable. How can what God brought into our lives be "morally evil," "wicked," "defective," "below standard," or "worthless"? It can't.

Yet, some of the definitions fall in a different vein. The Bereans were commended for searching scriptures to see if Paul's gospel was correct, or rather they were checking to see if it was a bad/inaccurate gospel. As Christians we are to "judge correctly" according to Jesus instruction in John 7:24. If we can "judge correctly" then there must be a way to judge incorrectly, or rather to judge in a "bad" way. These definitions are not the ones I speak of when I write:

As Christians, we **ARE NOT** given the

Right

Privilege

Honor

Authority

Position

Command

to ever label an event, occurrence, adventure, episode, or hardship as "bad."

We are to judge people as evil, if they are evil. A terrorist that kills innocent people is evil; A man who steals is a burglar; An unfaithful spouse is an adulterer.

We are within our walk as Christians to declare events, occurrences, adventures, episodes ... what they are. Your child dying of cancer is tragic. Your spouse beating you is criminal. Your father returning to a life of alcoholism is disappointing. The drop in the stock market is devastating to our retirement plans. Your house burning down is a great loss. The life-long missionary killed by the people he went to minister to is bewildering. A young man using street drugs to find peace is deceived.

Once while discussing this with a group of men, a participant shared how an old acquaintance of his had familiarity with this idea. He shared that this acquaintance would see his dog run over by a bus and exclaim, "Praise The Lord." *That's not what I'm talking about.* That response is, at best, delusional and at worst is disingenuous. Or, maybe the man was ready for a new dog.

The Contract

As Christians, we ARE NOT given the

Right

Privilege

Honor

Authority

Position

Command

to ever label an event, occurrence, adventure, episode, or hardship as "bad."

It's just not our job.

When we declare events as "bad," we are signing a contract. It's a supernatural contract. It's an agreement with another. That "another" presents himself anonymously at first. He may remain anonymous indefinitely as we live within the contract's stipulations. Here's an example of what that contract looks like:

I, _____, in light of
the aforementioned event happening, do
hereby declare the aforementioned event as
"bad," and thereunto invite the Enemy and his
minions to enter my world and give them authority
to bestow upon me any and all of the following in
combination and intensity as may serve their
purpose: fear, hatred, sleepless nights, anger,
wrath, selfishness, anxiety, lack of motivation, over work,
discord, impurity, addiction, obsessions, jealousy, immorality,
dissension, gossip, laziness, bitterness, ...

The print gets really small and the agreed to consequences
harder to discern and darker. This is not the contract a Christian
wants to sign. It's not a job we were given.

We are already under a contract. Our contract was sealed in
blood from a cross. In the spirit of full disclosure, this Holy
contract is also a contract with a lot of details that we don't
understand. I believe this is why we don't stay in this Holy
contract, because we don't fully understand the small print. Yet,
the "bad" contract is filled with small print we don't get. We are
often deceived and overlook that fact. In addition, as we live out
the Christian contract, we find there is more in this Holy
contract than a renewed relationship with God.

Part of a Christian's contract includes the following promise:

"And we know that in all things God works for
the good of those who love him, who have been
called according to his purpose" (Romans 8:28)

The English Standard Version of this verse reads this way:

"And we know that for those who love God all things work together for good, for those who are called according to his purpose"
(Romans 8:28 English Standard Version)

Our contract tells of a God who loves us and whom we love. We read here of a God who works good for us and that all things work for good. Do I always know where it's going? *No. I may be bewildered.* Might I have to endure physical discomfort? *Yep. It may hurt.* Will I have to go through the tears of losing something? *Yes.* Even Jesus cried. Will I understand why my retirement portfolio shrunk? *Maybe.* Your plans will have to be adjusted.

Someday in the future you may find yourself standing in front of an open refrigerator looking at a gallon of milk that's "do not drink past" date was last week. The milk has floating clods of white chunks on its surface. It is correct to judge that the milk is bad. Yet, if you chose to drink the milk and land up the next day in an ER, you'd be in error to call the event "bad." It would be correct to state the adventure is miserable, expensive and time consuming.

As Christians, we **ARE NOT** given the

Right

Privilege

Honor

Authority

Position

Command

to ever label an event, occurrence, adventure, episode, or hardship as "bad."

"It Was Good"

Genesis opens with God creating the universe. At the end of each day, God declared what He had just created as "good." Five times, He judged that what He had done was good. The sixth time He made a judgment call regarding His work; He called it "very good" (Genesis 1:31). Then He turned His creation over to his gardener, Adam.

I've heard many educated speakers speak on the bottom-line basis of why God's gardener failed in his job. The general consensus is that the fall was due to pride. I am no theologian; therefore, it might be unwise for me to doubt this position. Could it be that Adam's sin was more a trust issue than a pride issue? And, perhaps here I am just using a euphemism that ultimately leads to the same conclusion of a root of pride.

Adam had been given specific instructions on how to manage the business of the Garden. He was given only one thing not to do:

> "... do not eat from the tree of the knowledge of good and evil..." (Genesis 2:17)

Then along comes a salesman with a different gardening approach. This new approach called for eating what God had forbidden. Before Adam were now two different contracts bidding for his signature. Adam made a judgment call. Though God had declared and judged things repeatedly as good, Adam essentially declares that this not eating a certain fruit a "not good"/"bad" contract. His action shows that he declares this position to be bad. In so doing, Adam trusted Satan more than God. It was not Adam's job to declare it bad. In so doing, he signed a contract with a whole lot of small print that even affected his children and their offspring to this day.

Note the sequence: Options revealed→ lack of trust/faith→ doubt→ declaring something bad/signing a contract. Sin comes in when a job was taken that wasn't supposed to be taken ... declaring something bad. This is, at its heart, a trust issue. In the challenging adventures of life, we are faced with addressing how great is our trust in God.

For us to declare life issues as "bad" is to go against God's declaration that He is working these issues for our good. This isn't a mental/psychological adventure, a sort of "it's as bad or as good as I make it." It is more than just the belief that a positive attitude makes for a positive outcome. No, this is spiritual warfare stuff! It is what is spoken of in 2 Corinthians 10:3-5:

> "For though we live in the world, we do not wage war as the world does. The weapons we fight with are not the weapons of the world. On the contrary, they have divine power to demolish strongholds. We demolish arguments and every pretension that sets itself up against the knowledge of God, and we take captive every thought to make it obedient to Christ"

We are to come into agreement with God's declaration.

Judge Correctly

John 7 reveals an interesting interaction that occurred between Jesus and the religious leaders. Jesus had just healed a man on the Sabbath. An act the religious leaders had deemed bad. Jesus instructs them in His approach to life and includes very powerful command:

> "Stop judging by mere appearance, but instead judge correctly" (John 7:24)

So how does one "judge correctly?" By abiding, as we've discussed previously. If we are in proper relationship with God, our judgments will be correct. It would be wise to let Him do His job, and us to not do jobs not given to us.

As Christians, we **ARE NOT** given the

Right

Privilege

Honor

Authority

Position

Command

to ever label an event, occurrence, adventure, episode, or hardship as "bad."

John 7:24 has a subtle inference. That inference is that appearances can mislead or confuse or distract or tempt us.

Our Enemy would love for us to join Adam and declare events as bad. Our parents often taught us events could be judged as bad. Even without our parents teaching us, our nature is to often judge events as bad.

Event Reality

So, if we are not to label events as "bad," what then may they be called or labeled? Here are alternative terms to describe and package these areas of our life:

- afflicted
- hard/hardship
- trouble/troubled
- sorrowful
- challenging
- difficult
- beyond my level of expertise
- unexpected
- weird
- bewildering
- painful
- grievous
- miserable/misery
- tragic/an act of evil
- betrayed
- abandoned
- lonely

- heartbreaking
- tribulation
- turmoil
- odd timing
- disappointing
- surprising
- mysterious
- not understandable
- not forseen/unforseen

The death of your aunt in a car wreck is tragic and grievous. The theft of your car is an act of evil. Your 401-K going down with the market is mysterious and maybe unexpected and disappointing. Losing your finger in a chainsaw accident is painful. Your friend sharing a trusted secret is an act of betrayal. Are these events bad?

As Christians, we **ARE NOT** given the

Right

Privilege

Honor

Authority

Position

Command

to ever label an event, occurrence, adventure, episode, or hardship as "bad."

Some terms are not an option. "Not good" is the same as "bad." "Scary" implies that one has already deemed the situation bad and introduced a spirit of fear into the mix.

Some phrases work, yet I've found them personally so close to my old habits that I try to avoid them. Saying something "feels bad" is not the same as saying something is "bad." I try to avoid it. Something being "heartbreaking" is not the same as saying it's bad. Yet, it may reveal my heart was desirous of something other than God.

Job's View

Few characters in the Old Testament have been subjected to misery to the level that Job was. He lost his family (except his wife: that probably should tell us something about her. More on her in a minute). He lost his wealth. He lost his health. His friends were not only useless as encouragers, they piled more angst on him.

Job seems to be in a great position to make a call on the storms of life. His wife wanted to help him come to some conclusion on the matter. Her advice to him:

"Curse God and die!" (Job 2:9)

Read closely, Job's response:

"He replied, 'You are talking like a foolish woman. Shall we accept good from God, and not _____'" (Job 2:10)

I left the last part blank to drive home a point. Think about what the most logical next word or phrase should be. I've asked this question to scores of people. Far and away the most common answer is "bad." "Shall we accept good from God, and not <u>bad</u>." It seems like "bad" fits well in the blank. However, Job knew long ago that he wasn't in a position to take the job of declaring the events of his life "bad." No, the word he uses is "trouble." "Shall we accept good from God, and not **trouble**." Job wanted to live his hard and messed up life under a contract with God.

Chapter 42 of Job finds him having just spent a difficult time one-on-one with God. Here is part of Job's conclusion about the adventure he had been on:

> "I know that you (God) can do all things; no
> purpose of yours can be thwarted" (Job 42:2)

Job sees God as the one in charge, the one who declares "good and bad."

The habit of saying "that's bad" is a hard habit to break. I know. I've been there.

Discharge Plan

Self Examination:

* Why do you think we find it easy to label events occurrences, experiences of life and hardships as "bad?" What is going on in your life now that you have labeled "bad?"

- What phrases could be better used on that situation than the label of "bad"?

- What has been introduced into your life as a result of labeling a life event as "bad?"

- Recall an event in your life that you once called "bad," yet now you see God having used it to benefit you.

Treatment:

- If you've taken a job from God that He didn't give you, admit it and ask forgiveness.

- Verbally or in writing, inform the Enemy that you had no right to sign his contract. Therefore, it is an invalid contract and he has no rights to you.

- Start avoiding the old phrases that aren't true and replace them with true judgment statements.

Rehab:

> "And he died for all, that those who live should
> no longer live for themselves but for him who died
> for them and was raised again"
> (2 Corinthians 5:15)

> "Sovereign" by Chris Tomlin. *Burning Lights.*
> EMI Christian Music Group. 2013

CHAPTER FOUR

God Expectations

"The Lord is in his holy temple; let all the earth
be silent before him" (Habakkuk 2:20)

Life is hard.

Life is harder if we move through it without recognizing self imposed unrealities.

Doctor shows on TV are often comedies. It's interesting that a place where life and death issues are truly reviewed can serve as wonderful fodder for scriptwriters. Doctors are not immune to comedy bits in their real life room-to-room routines. I have several comedy bits that I "perform" as the opportunity arises. My poor staff has had to endure the reruns of my "skits" more often than they have seen *I Love Lucy* reruns.

One involves my response to a question that many patients pose as I listen to their heart sounds. As I listen, it's not unusual for a patient to jokingly ask me "Am I alive, Doc?" Little do they realize that question is my cue line. I will lift my stethoscope slowly and methodically. I pause with a very bothered look on my face. Then I respond, "Well, if you're not alive then your dead. If you're dead, you're either in heaven or hell. This doesn't feel like heaven, so you must be in hell. What's worse, I'm here with you!"

The misery spoken of in my office behind a closed exam room door is often of such a level that I understand why someone coined the term, "hell on earth." It's sad the level of distress in the world. Sadder still is when those persistent battles open up new fronts of guilt, second guessing, feelings of failure and self-condemnation.

If we buy into the lie that we should be "handling it," and yet we know we are not handling it, the world becomes a dark lonely place of shame, doubt and defeat. It leads to social game playing. We surely don't want our "witness" destroyed by letting those around us know we aren't doing very well. So we put on the plastic smile, the fake joy, the shallow conversation (don't get too close or deep, one can only hide for a short time.) Maybe we go to the other extreme. Wearing our misery as a distress signal hoping someone has a way to save us.

It seems we've forgotten that we are in a battle, a supernatural spiritual battle with a diabolical Enemy. His methods are many. He strives to confuse. He longs to bewilder. He's great at distracting. His goal is to win at any cost or method. He'll make up verses. I suppose you've guessed by now that I think Grandma's Verse is from the Gates of Hell.

The Enemy will take a powerful verse like Philippians 4:13 and use it as a condemnation "tool." He will say, "You sure don't seem to be doing 'everything' because the outcomes don't look too spiritually impressive."

Here, I have to give kudos to the writings of John Eldridge. He has greatly enlightened me on the Enemy's tactics. Especially as it relates to how we make false "agreements." Others have referred to these as "worldly agreements" or "non-Biblical agreements."

We often judge our "doing everything" by how the outcome measures up to our predetermined/expected outcome. John Eldridge refers to these as "agreements." These are powerful weapons that the Enemy will use on us. We are also at fault because an agreement has to be agreed to by us. Here's an example of how an agreement can mess with us.

Suppose a friend invites you to come over for roast beef dinner tonight. If I were to get you to write down on a sheet of paper what you anticipate to be on your plate that night, here's what you might write: Roast beef, potatoes, green beans, rolls and a salad. Where did that list come from? Your friend only said that you were having roast beef. Those other foods you listed were your agreements as to what should be included with a roast beef dinner. That's not an unrealistic agreement based on American culture and tradition.

Now, suppose you grew up in a place that when you had roast beef there was only roast beef and green beans. If I invited you over and we had all those other things listed above, you'd end up with probably one of two extreme emotions due to your agreement that the roast beef only needed green beans as a side item. First, you might be filled with a Thanksgiving-like joy seeing the bounty of food on your plate. You'd think. "I must be a special person to have all the items fixed for me." No, that would be joy based on false assumptions. You're not that special and your false joy is at risk when you find out you're not special. Or you might be on the other side of the emotional spectrum. You might ponder, "Why is there so much on my plate. They must want something from me!!" That interpretation would steal the joy of the meal from you as you waited for someone to tell you what they want from you.

Now, let's consider what if you, with your Americanized big meal expectations, went to the less hefty meal maker for dinner? You walk in and there on your plate is just roast beef and green beans. Once more, one of two extreme emotions might be present. I label one "male" pattern response and one "female" pattern response. I will let you guess which is which. First, you might instantly think, "That's it! Where are my potatoes and rolls?" Your expectations of a large meal have stolen your joy over a meal that 95% of the world would be thrilled to be eating. Or you might think, "Oh my! Did I misunderstand? Was I supposed to bring the potatoes and the rolls?" Once again, most of the world would sit down and joyfully eat the roast beef and green beans. Yet, you endure your meal pondering how you messed up by not bringing potatoes and rolls. Both "male" and "female" responses would be wrong. Your host only serves beans with roast. Your agreement has led you to miseries that only exist in you.

In the same way our agreements of expected spiritual outcomes in life can lead us to joyless experience of our time here on earth. How can we avoid this spiritual pitfall?

The first step is to realize that God isn't freaking out in heaven. Habakkuk 2:20 states, "But the Lord is in his holy temple; let all the earth be silent before him." In other words, He's got this. He's got you. Psalm 4:8 states, "I will lie down and sleep in peace, for you alone, O Lord, make me dwell in safety."

Unexpected Outcomes

Scripture is full of people who, from all accounts, did the right thing, at the right time, for the right reason. Yet, the outcomes were unexpected.

Let's take a look at Joseph whose story is found in Genesis 37-50. Genesis 39 finds Joseph as a slave in Egypt. He is the slave of a man named Potiphar. Potiphar's wife was attracted to Joseph and made advances toward him. This was a "day-after-day" interaction. Joseph gives his reasons for not agreeing to her invitation to have an affair. Let's pick up the story in verse 8:

> "But he (Joseph) refused. 'With me in charge,' he told her, 'my master does not concern himself with anything in the house; everything he owns he has entrusted to my care. No one is greater in this house than I am. My master has withheld nothing from me except you, because you are his wife. How then could I do such a wicked thing and sin against God?' And though she spoke to Joseph day after day, he refused to go to bed with her or even be with her" (Genesis 39:8-10)

So here's Joseph doing the right thing, at the right time, for the right reason. I can imagine that he was spending a lot of time in the Ol' PAUSE, EXAMINE YOUR MOTIVE, ASK abiding land! What does this level of loyalty and God-like living get him? Verses 11-20 reveal that when he rebuffed her one more time than she could stand, she framed him for attempted rape and had him thrown in prison.

We could examine many other individuals in scripture and see unexpected outcomes from abiding within God's principles and precepts. The list would include: Jeremiah, Stephen, Paul, John the Baptist and Job to name a few.

The Three "D's" of God-Directed Discomfort

Reading of Godly people enduring discomfort is a challenge to the theology of many. It seems most would have no trouble with discomfort if it related to some sinful act. Yet, God has demonstrated in scripture His use of discomfort in three ways: Discipline, Development, and Deployment. (Kudos again to my friend John Riddle for his insight here. He must have some Baptist preacher side in him since they all begin with the same letter.)

Discipline

This "D" is the one most people understand a Holy God using. It represents a response to an act of disobedience. Most of us know when we are being disciplined. Each of the "D's" actually comes with God-given emotions to let us know which "D" we are experiencing. For discipline, that emotional marker is in the land of regret. The person in the midst of discipline knows why he is there unless he is in major denial. The Biblical poster child of this "D" could be Jonah. Instructed by God to head in one direction, Jonah heads the opposite way. Soon he finds himself in the belly of a fish with an ocean full of regret.

Development

This "D" seems to be where most Christians dwell while at the same time longing for it to be done with. The emotional marker for development would be in the land of puzzlement and its emotional cousins. The person in development might ask, "Why is this happening?"; "When will this adventure end?"; "How can I get out of here?" Even the more insightful believer will desire escape from development's lesson. The poster child here could be David. His life was full of great times of puzzling struggle that many of the Psalms attest to.

Deployment

This "D" seems to be the one where God would have us dwell. The emotional marker for deployment is peace or joy. The person in deployment is aware of his situation. He is not in denial. In spite of the gravity or the depth of the misery or of impending peril, he is still pointing those around him to God. The poster child here would most certainly be the Apostle Paul. Though put in prison for the Gospel, he rejoices in the opportunity to tell his jailors of God's grace.

Will I have to experience the three "D's?" It's unavoidable. Call them what they are. You made a sinful choice and now you bear up under discipline. Your home you worked thousands of hours to build is destroyed by a tornado. You are developing a new perspective of life. You are fired because of your Christian beliefs. Welcome to the beautiful land of unemployed deployment. Beware calling the occurrences "bad." Only God gets the job that I try to assume when I label these "bad."

These "D's" can occasionally be seen happening together. I find God is into the multitasking thing. A person being disciplined can at some level deploy knowledge of God's Holiness to others (i.e. the thief on the cross next to Jesus). Hopefully, the discipline in that individual will develop them. Psalm 51 reveals David deep in the land of discipline, writing of his development and that Psalm is still today deploying knowledge of God.

Satan is not unaware of the "D's" employed by God. He can't stop God, however Satan does try to pervert the process for his own gain. Against the person who is being disciplined, the Enemy may introduce a spirit of shame or guilt. The person God is developing is where Satan attacks with doubt and the temptation to lose faith in God. People in the deployment "D" often are assailed with second-guessing and narrowing of eternal vision. He has a goal to bring discouragement when the storms of deployment arise. He longs for us to deem hardships in life as "bad." In so doing, we put a sense of unredeemable finality with life's difficulties. Yet, God is The God of redemption. We don't have to fear hardships.

Dog Nights

The following story's woes pale when compared to the level of misery experienced elsewhere in life. Yet, its lesson is one of the top ten I've ever learned.

One of the great mysteries of life is why do all of a dog owner's neighbors awaken to a dog's 2AM barking and yet the dog's owner hears nothing? Anyone who has lost sleep due to a disturbing canine can understand my frustration many years ago, when I lived this mystery.

I value my sleep. There's something about being rested and thinking clearly that I find makes my days run a little smoother. Brookshire Lane in Pelham, Alabama, where I lived at the time of this life lesson, was normally a quiet street. Then, one night a neighbor's dog decided to blast away the peaceful quiet. After several rounds of dog-disturbed nights, I began to contemplate my options to resolve the situation. Though the mature thing would have been to speak to the neighbor, I pondered darker avenues. (At this stage in my life, I suppose I was not mature enough to handle minor conflict.) Some hydrocodone left over from a family member's recent surgery could do the job. A few of those suckers strategically placed in a hot dog and tossed over a fence would serve my sleepy neighbor's and me well.

Yet, before I could implement this plan, I was challenged with the understanding that God was aware of my dog-inflicted insomnia. He wasn't freaking out over my situation. He also, as evidenced by my accumulating hours of sleep deprivation, wasn't willing to take this dog out of my life with a quick bolt of lighting. He was doing something here.

I had been mentored in the PAUSE, EXAMINE YOUR MOTIVES, ASK steps of abiding. Therefore, before pursuing my illegal solution, I decided to follow those steps in this situation and see where God would lead me. You'd think that would please God enough for Him to send that bolt of lighting. It apparently wasn't. The dog continued its alarm. I continued to awaken.

On those nights, God would sometimes lead me to pray for my family and friends. Other times He led me to read scripture. During this time, I was reading an autobiography of a noted Christian leader. I was often led to pick it up and read another chapter. Sometimes He led me to just worship.

A beautiful thing happened. I grew. I grew closer to God. I had more joy in the night. The day after I would be awakened were filled with energy and clarity of thought even though I had missed out on several hours of sleep. I soon began to celebrate and praise God for the nights the dog would awaken me. The fruit of those nights was so powerful.

Eventually, I would, upon lying down in bed for the night, pray for God to use the dog to awaken me! I enjoyed my nighttime rendezvous with God.

And then, the dog stopped barking. That segment of my journey was done. I don't know why the dog stopped. Maybe the Enemy's plans to use the dog to mess with me backfired. Maybe some other tired neighbor put some old hydrocodone to use.

Yes, we are wrong in labeling hardships as bad. Even more disconcerting is the idea that our avoiding certain misery could bring us in opposition to God's very well developed plans!

Discharge Plan

Self Examination:

- What "worldly/non-Biblical agreement" is stealing your joy at this time?

- When do "worldly/non-Biblical agreements" become our idols?

- Remember a time when you were disciplined.

- Remember a time when you were developed.

- Remember a time when you were deployed

- Have you ever had a time where you confuse "development" with "discipline?" Where did that lead to emotionally/spiritually?

- Which of the three "D's" do you find yourself in now?

- What is the hardest aspect of each "D?"

- Satan seeks to steal, kill, and destroy. Which "D" is he trying to pervert to his benefit instead of having the "D" benefit you? How is he doing this?

Treatment:

- Search scripture related to your "worldly/non-Biblical agreements" to bring them in line with God.

- Seek for ways to move your life struggles into deployment mode.

Rehab:

"But seek first his kingdom and his righteousness, and all these things will be given to you as well." Matthew 6:33 (NIV)

"Protest to Praise" by Downhere. *Downhere.* Word Records. 2001

"

CHAPTER FIVE

"BTABS"

"The younger one said to his father, 'Father, give me my share of the estate.' So he divided his property between them" (Luke 15:12)

Life is hard.

Life is harder if you live trying to avoid "bad" events.

We are an acrostic driven world. This is especially true in the field of medicine.

PTSD = Post Traumatic Stress Disorder

ARDS = Adult Respiratory Distress Syndrome

HIV = Human Immune Virus

GERD = Gastro Esophageal Reflux Disorder

OBTW = Oh, By The Way

Okay, this last one I made up for my office notes to let me know the patient surprised me with some other issue they wanted to address but didn't tell my receptionist while making the appointment. OBTW's help me run behind.

I think we humans often live life suffering from BTABS. BTABS ("be tabs") stands for "Bad Thing Avoidance Behavior Syndrome." It's one of the most devastating effects of taking on the job of labeling things as "bad." It typically starts with mild symptoms that we will review below. It is progressive, though many reach a steady state of BTABS. The following is an example of that progression.

Life is full of choices. This is true for Christians and non-Christians alike. In our example here, we will look at someone addressing choices in the "standard" Christian way. When faced with a choice they gather all the information about the choice. They pray about the options available. They fast. They pray. They PAUSE, EXAMINE THEIR MOTIVES and ASK. They seek out expert advice. Godly mentors are questioned as to their take on the situation. Then the decision is made.

In our example today, let's have a pondering Christian trying to choose between three options: "A," "B," or "C" (This could be three different houses to buy; three job offers; three schools to send the children to, and so forth.) So, our faithful Christian employs the standard "how" in making a Christ-like decision model as noted above. Choice "A" is selected.

If you recall, it's a cursed and broken world. Choice "A" has some hard issues that come to light. (The house basement floods easily; the new job comes with a boss who is a jerk; the children's new classroom has a bully after them.) If our pondering Christian takes on the job of labeling these issues as "bad," then the inclination is to look back over their shoulder and bemoan that they should have chosen "B" or "C"!

However, they ARE in the land of "A" and now new choices appear: "D," "E," and "F" (move to another house/stay/sue the real estate agency; deal with the boss/change jobs again/report the new boss to superiors; have your child learn karate/change school/meet with the teacher.) Once more, the "standard" Christian methods are employed. This time the decision is made for "E" (One really should always choose the middle choice anyway, right?)

Guess what's in the domain of "E"? Hardships, surprises, disappointment, which, in our example, the Christian will label as "bad." Then they will ponder as to why they didn't choose "D" or "F" and how much better it would have been if they had made a different choice. They may begin to resent their "experts" and Godly mentors. They see the "wonderful" life of those who chose "B" or "F" and the seeds of jealousy and envy are planted. (They don't realize those who chose "B" or "F" are hiding their life's misery from those who chose the other options.)

And now, living in the sphere of "E," our poor decision-maker is faced with still more options: Choice #1, Choice #2, or Choice #3. Confidence that was unsteady in the beginning is now truly in dire straights. Doubt permeates almost every area of their life. Sleep is disrupted. Relationships are strained. In regards to deciding between #1, #2 or #3, our hero becomes the proverbial "deer in the headlights" character: frozen with fear, self-doubt, loss of faith, second guessing, bitterness, blaming, seemingly in dire need of a Xanax or Prozac.

BTABS Origin

The debate around the origin of trying to avoid bad things is the same as many other medical syndromes/illnesses: is it an acquired problem (environmentally induced/how we were nurtured growing up) or is it something we are born with (genetics/our nature)? It's the ol' "nature verses nurture" quandary.

I recall as a parent how I often "encouraged" my children with words such as, "If you don't pass that test it will be bad." Or, "Putting that dent in the car was bad." Or, "Not getting accepted to that organization is bad." "Showing up late is bad." I infected my children with the concept of me being the one to decide an event's "badness." Or, perhaps, I wasn't as much infecting them as throwing gas on a fire that smolders in all of us.

In Genesis 3, we find the story of Adam and Eve and the first sin. That first sin had at its root this propensity for humans to take a job that was not ours. Satan essentially tells Adam and Eve that God is not giving all the correct info. The temptation is for them to see this as a bad deal and take a job that was not theirs. Adam "signs the contract" that in effect says that in light of him not being "like God," he, Adam, deems the situation bad and therefore will sign on with Satan as to a better way to be like God. Adam chose the nature of sin and that nature was passed on to us.

Therefore, it seems, Bad Thing Avoidance Behavior Syndrome, like most sin, has both a nature and a nurture component.

Skateboard Dilemmas

Two little boys named Johnny are standing in a road going down a gently sloping hill. Each has their mother beside him. Each has a skateboard in hand.

Johnny #1's mother looks lovingly at him. She says, "Johnny, you've loved skateboarding so far. But, you've been doing it on level parking lots. When you begin going down this hill you will start moving faster and faster. At some point, you will fall off the skateboard and probably get hurt. Let's go play on the swings."

Johnny #2's mother looks lovingly at him. She says, "Johnny, you've loved skateboarding so far. But, you've been doing it on level parking lots. When you begin going down this hill you will start moving faster and faster. At some point, you will fall off the skateboard and probably get hurt. But, I brought some Band-Aids, ace wraps, ice packs and we have Blue Cross insurance. Go for it son!"

Both moms love their Johnny.

Both moms are correct that their Johnny will fall.

Both moms are correct that their Johnny will be injured.

Both Johnnies hear the same thing, to this point.

When Johnny#1's mom suggests that he avoid pain and injury, he hears things mom never intended. He hears, "You will fail." He hears, "You need to avoid failure because it is bad." He hears, "You can't handle failure." And worst of all, somewhere in his spirit, he hears, "God can't handle your failure."

I don't claim to be a prophet. However, after 30 years in medicine, I can give you a pretty good idea of where Johnny #1 is headed. He will be unlikely to overachieve in school. He'll be timid at some level. He will act out his plugged-up spirit of adventure with such outbursts of anger that few will see his underlying timidity. He will avoid risk for a while. The pent-up frustration will periodically explode into YouTube worthy "What was he thinking video" moments. He will be less likely to take a chance on love, asking a girl out is too risky. He will escape into virtual realities. (Paint balls hurt and can put your eye out! A video game bullet never breaks the skin.) He will be 26 years old in his parent's basement apartment. There he will be playing games with a stranger 12,000 miles a way and getting madder at the poor play of his virtual teammate than he got at the perpetrators in the dog abuse TV program he saw last night. And, his relationship with God will suck. He will lead a life of "playing it safe."

When Johnny #2's mom suggests that the pain and failure are worth it, if she's as wise as I'd hope, she understands what he hears. He hears, "You will fail," the same as Johnny #1. But, then the other messages are very different. He hears, "There's no need to avoid pain and failure, good is there." He hears, "You'll survive." And, best of all, somewhere in his spirit, he hears, "You'll survive because God has got this."

I don't claim to be a prophet. However, after 30 years in medicine I can give you a pretty good idea of where Johnny #2 is headed. He WILL break his arm skateboarding. He will cry at first and then in awhile he will laugh. And, he will learn. And, mythic stories will become of the day he broke his arm. Oh, it was a grand adventure! He will likely overachieve in school. He will be aggressive, yet wise in the chances he takes. He will get lawns to mow in the summer even though he knows he could cut his foot off or be overtaken by yellow jackets. He will ask a girl out on a date. He will experience "puppy love." She will move to another state. He will hurt. He will ask another girl out on a date. Someday he will marry some girl he asked out. They will brave having children. He will start his own business even though he knows that 2 out of 3 young businesses like his fail. And, he will be desperate to stay close to God. He will lead a life of adventure, taking appropriate safe guards because he's not stupid.

There seems to be a logarithmic principle in the spiritual realm. Sin seems to lead to more sin, which leads to more impactful sin. Now sin is sin in God's eye. That's not what I'm referring to. For example, most embezzlers don't begin with a $100,000 embezzlement scheme. They began by taking a few pens. Then maybe they took some money from the petty cash box. Then they diverted some cash payments to their pocket. Then they work on the big money. Johnny #1's mom deemed something bad. Then Johnny #1 agreed things could be bad. Then he played it safe and started "hiding his talents" (Check out the story of the men in Matthew 25 who were given responsibilities. Note the one who dared nothing. He was severely condemned for living a life of BTABS.)

Nurturing the Nature

The farm where I was raised in Cullman County in north central Alabama is situated in a land of slow rolling hills. The land has the capacity to handle diverse agricultural endeavors. Chicken houses are a major driving force in the economy today. During my formative years, it was a county of cotton, soybean, hay, corn, and cattle. My father had decided we would spend more energy on cattle and hay baling with a little gardening on the side. Four sons will motivate a man to do something to keep those young men busy, make a better living and teach some life lessons. He put together a little hay baling enterprise. We cut hay, raked hay, baled hay, hauled hay, put hay in barns, and (worst of all) put hay in barn lofts. We baled up to 25,000 bales a summer. These were the old "square" bales that were designed for a man to lift, throw, and stack on a truck or trailer and haul to the barn. Then to unstack them, throw them up in the loft and stack them again.

If a parent wants to motivate their child to attend college, plant their butt on a no air-conditioned Massie Ferguson 135 tractor in Cullman County on a 101-degree day in August and afterwards have him pick up, haul and barn 500 bales of hay along with his three tired, irritable brothers. My parents helped pay for some of my college. I paid for most of it. I was motivated.

The Apostle Paul tried a farming analogy. In so doing, he demonstrated that he must've been a city boy. He wrote in 1 Corinthians 3 of how different individuals contributed to the growing of God's kingdom. His farming analogy spoke of some individuals planting, others watering, and then God making things grow. Having grown up on a farm, I noticed Paul skipped a step. Yes, a seed is planted. Then the seed will need water to grow. In addition, after the seed is planted, farmers know to put fertilizer on seeded ground. Paul missed speaking of the fertilizer step. In our garden, we would often use manure as a cheap "home grown" fertilizer. I often think of my place in the growth of God's kingdom like the manure spreader. What I do is kinda messy and stinks but somehow God can use what I do.

The seed (nature) of sin was planted in us years ago by Adam's choice. We are new creatures in Christ but will not have all of our old nature cleared until heaven. During our time here on earth we can water and fertilize (nurture) that old Adamic seed or the seed of Christ in us. As Johnnies' mothers demonstrated, we can nurture the seeds of sin or the seeds of righteousness. The manure of life has the potential to bring forth the fruit of the Spirit.

There are many battlefronts in life. We may have the option to avoid some battles. Most times, we will be engaged in the battles of life. The two most basic battlefronts are within ourselves and with the world around us. First, we will address the battles within ourselves (Chapters 6-8) and after that, we will take on the conflicts the world brings our way (Chapter 9).

Discharge Plan

Self Examination:

- What hard event or decision made in your past still harshly affects your life?

- What painful/hard aspect of life do you try to avoid?

- What next step, adventure, event or decision are you avoiding because you are trying to circumvent a potentially "bad" life experience?

- Who caused/causes the most pain/scaring in your life?

Treatment:

- Forgive yourself and others for those acts/decisions that come to mind through the self examination questions.

- Resolve to live in the present, not in the past.

- Resolve to move boldly through the next adventure.

Rehab:

> "Keep this Book of the Law always on your lips; meditate on it day and night, so that you may be careful to do everything written in it. Then you will be prosperous and successful. Have I not

commanded you? Be strong and courageous. Do not be afraid; do not be discouraged, for the LORD your God will be with you wherever you go." Joshua 1:8-9 (NIV)

"It is Well With My Soul" by Horatio G. Spafford (1828-1888)

CHAPTER SIX

Muddy Water

"So God created man in his own image, in the image of God He created him; male and female He created them" (Genesis 1:27)

Life is hard.

Life is harder if you're messed up.

The story is often told of how the treasury department trains its employees to spot a counterfeit bill. They don't train them by studying the different methods and techniques of counterfeiters. Those methods and techniques are ever-changing and the crooks will inevitably stay one step ahead of the law.

The treasury department has its employees study the real bill. They become experts at what the real bill looks like. Therefore, they become experts on what is real and what is counterfeit.

If we are to understand how to stop taking jobs from God that aren't ours, or buying into half-truths told to us, we must first understand what God did when He made humans. A look at His overall creation reveals two basic levels of creation: living things and non-living things. Within the category of living things, we find three levels of His creative work. These three levels could be categorized as:

- Those living creatures with a body only;

- Those living creatures with a body and soul;

- Those living creatures with a body, soul, and spirit.

In the first category, those with a body only, we would find trees, grass, seaweed, corn, for example.

The second category holds those creatures with body and soul. (Many people understandably use the term soul and spirit interchangeably. My definition here for soul includes that part of a creature that includes emotions, mind, and will. I will define the word spirit in a moment.) In this category, for example, we would find horses, dogs, rhinos, birds and turtles.

The last category is made up of creatures with body, soul, and spirit. Spirit here refers to that unique aspect that would make a creature have the image of God. Only one such creature is found in scripture with that characteristic: man. (See Genesis 1:26-27.)

Pathology/illness can exist within each category and gets more complicated as one moves from the first to the third level. For example, a tree struck by a car will have its bark mangled or its limbs broken and thus would need aid in healing that damage. Yet, there is no need to sit down with the tree and calm its fears of death or subsequent bug infestation. The tree knows nothing of forgiving the driver.

A dog struck by a car will also possibly have its bark mangled (Sorry, I just couldn't pass that one up) or a limb broken. Yet, now in addition to giving aid to heal the damage, it would be appropriate to spend time addressing the dog's emotions of fear, change his will to not bite the driver, and teach his mind how to respond to moving cars. Dogs can also be so emotionally distraught from the recent death of an owner that its body becomes affected. It may lose its appetite, develop diarrhea as physical/body pathology resulting from its soul illness/sadness.

The Three-Legged Stool

Being a physician is a complicated and hard job. It's one of those understood aspects of being a physician. Another understood aspect of being a physician is that you don't speak of how complicated and hard the job is. I guess the idea is who wants to hear a whiny doctor? One more understood aspect of being a doc is that you don't speak of the main reason the job is so complicated and hard. It's complicated and hard because we have to deal with patients. That doesn't sound very kind and compassionate. I think in the very small print of the Hippocratic oath it says something about don't even go there, guys and gals.

Often the hardest part of patient care is finding out what level of their being is the primary source of pathology, and what are secondary symptoms. Many years ago, I developed a little introductory story to help my patients see the dilemma we faced. Initially, I used the story to help certain patients see that their physical symptoms were actually secondary to emotional battles. I call it my "Three Legged Stool Approach."

I have the classic four-legged rolling stool found in most doctors' offices. I point out to patients that a four-legged stool is quite sturdy. Even if one leg is broken or poorly functioning, I could simply move over - above the other three legs - and find the three-legged version stable. However, if a three-legged stool has one dysfunctional leg, the whole stool is dysfunctional.

I approach patients as if they are a three-legged stool. One leg is their body/physical component. The second leg is their soul (mind/will/emotions) component. The last leg is their spirit component. Then I share the following with the patient in order to demonstrate the interplay between the components. My goal is to get them to explore contributions from each component. Here's the story:

"Suppose upon leaving my office you pull out of my drive onto the main road and your car is struck by a big garbage truck. The damage is such that your arm has you trapped and then a fire breaks out in the car. I happen to keep a machete at my office and that day it comes in handy to cut off your arm. The car burns up your trapped arm; you are saved. We ship you off to the hospital for emergency surgery.

"Your primary problem that day is a physical/body one. The wound of your amputated arm needs fixing. Yet, you have some real secondary problems. Looking at the soul (emotional/mind/will) component, your emotions are ablaze pondering, 'Does anybody find a one arm person attractive?'; 'How can I play ball with my nephew if I only have one arm?'; 'I wish I could get my hand on that truck driver!' And your spirit component yells up at God, 'Why me? Why not the murderer or the pedophile?'

"Two months go by. You're back home recovering on your front porch with your only true friend in the world, your dog. He sees a squirrel in the yard and gives chase only to run out in front of the same garbage truck that hit you two months before. It's an ugly dog-squashing scene. Your primary problem now is on the soul (emotional/mind/will) component. Heavy grief and despair are present. Yet, once again, the other components have very real secondary manifestations. Physically, if I were to come up to you at that moment, I might find you vomiting and misinterpret your symptoms as a stomach virus rather than you just saw your dog get killed. On the other hand, you might be hyperventilating and I'd be led to pursue the physical possibilities of a blood clot after your recent surgeries. And, then there would be the secondary spiritual battles as you question how a loving God could let a dog die when there are so many squirrels that could have been hit.

"Let's change the storyline a little. Now we're going to make the spirit component the primary dysfunction. Let's say we have an 18-year-old young man who, as the Ol' Baptist preacher would say, is 'spiritually and morally bankrupt.' He sees no God, has no use for the Bible, and does what his hormones tell him to do. This fella heads off to college. You know that, even though his primary problem is spiritual, he's gonna have some secondary body problems. He's going to get a broken arm after hitting a tree while driving drunk. He's gonna get an STD. He's gonna get some buckshot in his rear-end from the daddy of someone he's been messin' with! He may not have the secondary soul (mind/will/emotion) component symptoms until 25 years later. That's when he's putting his precious little daughter into her car headed for college. He realizes there are 18 year-old boys out there like he was. Now he can't sleep at night. He obsessively calls his princess asking her who her male friends are, what are their names, where are they from. She's even calling the family doctor about her dad, and tells the doctor she thinks her dad is going crazy!"

Our three-component nature presents many opportunities to treat some very real and disturbing secondary issues and miss the primary problem. It's like treating the fever component of a deadly pneumonia with Tylenol and not giving antibiotics for the infection. I have used this story for years to encourage patients with physical symptoms to be open to the possibility that those were secondary issues to emotional/mind/will issues.

It helped break down barriers that a lot of people had that blocked their use of medicine and counseling.

The three-legged stool has also served as a useful tool for reminding the patient and me that the process of diagnosing and treating is a complicated one. Because secondary pathology **is** secondary is not a reason to ignore it or not treat it. Sometimes the immediate danger of a secondary issue should take priority. A suicidal patient's bleeding wounds need to be fixed before one addresses the spirit and soul issues. The following pages will look at each component individually in regards to healthy maintenance, diagnosis, and treatment. When dealing with real life situations, multitasking is the overriding theme.

Spirit Priority

All word pictures breakdown at some point. That is true of my three-legged stool analogy. A stool has all three legs on an equal plane. Not so, in regards to how God created man.

The heart is a unique organ. It is a muscle that persistently works with very little time for rest. It is a symphony of electricity, fluid dynamics, valve technology and mechanical intricacy. A small area of the heart known as the sinus node orchestrates its activity. The sinus node begins the heart beat process by sending out an electrical signal that leads to heart muscle constriction. This constriction essentially causes the heart to collapse in on itself. The inside of the heart is arranged with two sets of two inline chambers. These chambers are filled with fluid (blood). As the muscle constricts, pressure within the chambers increases causing the fluid within to seek escape to lower pressure areas. The potential escape routes have valves at their location. As the fluid pressure increases, some of these valves close while others open, thereby defining which way the fluid will flow. The electrical instructions fire in the heart's upper two chambers first. Moments later the lower chambers fire. The muscles relax and the chambers fill with fluid as directed by the valves. The process creates a flow of blood through the heart. The average heart rate at rest is 75 beats per minute. The above process took less than one second. Then it repeats the process again. If the sinus node leads, the end results are healthy heart dynamics. The heart may still work if the node doesn't lead, but not as it was designed to function.

So it is with body, soul, and spirit. Any of the three may lead in a person's life. But, we were designed to be led by our spirit. More specifically, we were to lead a spirit led life that takes its lead from God. We are designed to function best when the Holy Spirit is our "sinus node" of life.

Worldly Misleadings

There should be a great deal of respect given to our capacity to be messed up and not even realize it. My father's most famous warning to me growing up was, "The easiest person in the world to fool is yourself." Living life based on foundational misinformation may or may not cause any immediate harm. But, it will eventually. Fooling ourselves seems fairly easy. It's made all the easier when others contribute to our misinformation.

There are realities to life. One of those realties is that there is a spiritual part of us. Now, here is an incredible irony of our world: Hollywood takes reality and makes a fictional movie about this reality. If a person chooses to live out their life in that reality that Hollywood depicted as fiction, that person is seen as not being in touch with reality.

So, Hollywood and the world delve into the supernatural thereby functionally and socially deeming the supernatural as not a pragmatic reality for people to find life's purpose. Nor is the spirit part of us seen as playing a role in the pathologies of our life. The body, mind, will, and emotion are, per their considerations, the only realities that need be addressed in the miseries found in people's lives.

Ignoring the supernatural often has no immediate outward symptoms. And, here's another irony: this lack of immediate symptoms is often used as further evidence of the supernatural's non-impact on an individual, i.e. it's not a real part of who they are. As such, when symptoms do occur they are viewed as being related only to body/mind/will/emotion issues, because those are real (versus the "unreality" of the spirit nature of man). Maybe there is reason treatments for those areas have such poor results.

We cannot just treat ourselves as we would treat an ill tree. Nor is it wise to treat ourselves as we would other animals. Genesis 1:27 tells us, "So God created mankind in his own image, in the image of God he created them: male and female he created them." In the ensuing centuries, He "developed" an owner's manual for His creation: The Bible. It's a complicated book in many respects, however, its truths are not beyond our capacity to glean. We just need to keep asking more questions.

In life, we are going to follow an "owner's" manual. It may be one we come up with on our own; Or, it may come from the world and others. Or, it will be the Bible, God's written guide for us.

Discharge Plan

Self Examination:

- Recall a time when you let body, or mind, or emotions, or will, lead instead of a God-directed spirit. What were the results?
- Recall a time when you felt one area of who you are (body, soul and spirit) as the main problem and you discovered it was a secondary symptom.
- Why are we resistant to looking beyond our physical symptoms for soul and spirit causes?
- Why does Hollywood/the world have such an impact on our approach to life?
- What is the most common "owner's manual" used by you?
- When was the last time you read all the way through your Bible? (If never, what barriers need to be overcome?)

Treatment:

- Ask God to give you discernment into identifying the primary areas of struggles that you need to address.
- Make a commitment to spend more time reading and studying the Bible.
- Commit to read all the way through the Bible.

Rehab:

"I praise you because I am fearfully and wonderfully made; your works are wonderful, I know that full well" (Psalm 139:14)

"We Are Not as Strong as We Think We Are" by Rich Mullen. *Songs*. Reunion Records. 1996

CHAPTER SEVEN

Dam Fixing

"For though we live in the world, we do not wage war as the world does. The weapons we fight with are not the weapons of the world. On the contrary, they have divine power to demolish strongholds. We demolish arguments and every pretention that sets itself up against the knowledge of God, and we take captive every thought to make it obedient to Christ" (2 Corinthians 10:3-5)

Life is hard.

Life is harder if you keep making the same mistakes.

Charlie Brown's teacher and parents sounded the same to me as the patient sitting in front of me.

"Wa wa waaaa waw waak wak waaak wa wak wa waaaaaaaa wakawa wak waaaak wa wa wa wa wa wak waaaak."

When I realized this, I was overcome by guilt at my lack of professionalism so I refocused to hear more clearly.

Still, all I could hear was, "Wa wa waaaa waw waak wak waaak wa wak wa waaaaaaaa wakawa wak waaaak wa wa wa wa wa wak waaaak." I tried to assuage my guilt by rationalizing that I was tired. I doubled up on my focus. Focus, Doug. Foooooocus!!!!

Still there: "Wa wa waaaa waw waak wak waaak wa wak wa waaaaaaaa wakawa wak waaaak wa wa wa wa wa wak waaaak." Then the cause of this occurred to me. This lady had been a patient of mine for over 20 years. It was a life filled with much misery, trials and tribulations that left her damaged in body, soul, and spirit. She had been to multiple doctors and taken most every medicine available to address her life issues. Her chart was literally fifteen inches thick. I was holding a folder with her name on it that was also labeled chart 8 of 8 for her. Today she was building chapter 287. But, this chapter was eerily similar to chapters 33 and 46 and 88 and 135 and 157-192 and 216 and 244.

As the "wak waaa wa waa" trailed off into my brain's background noise I pondered two things, neither of which I'm proud to share. First, was that of seeing myself as that poor boy at the leaking dam sticking his fingers in leaking holes waiting for the dam fixers to show up and rescue this lady and me. Fingers! Heck, with this lady I was using my feet, toes and elbows. And, still there were leaks.

"Wa waaa waaak wak wa."

The second thought was worse. It was the reassurance to myself that I'd only have to do this for ten or fifteen more years then the next fat-fingered doctor can take my place because there apparently was no fixing this dam!

Such remorse over having those ugly thoughts roaming my mind must have led me to a great urge to confess my unprofessionalism. In a moment of poorly thought out vulnerability, I proceeded to tell the one person closest at hand, the lady HERSELF! I confessed it all: the hearing "waaak wa waaaa wa," the inability to focus on her true words, the boy at the dam analogy, and finally my goal of easing my misery by handing her off to the next doctor in a few years.

God is so gracious. He is there when we most need him. He showed up for me that day, at that moment. Lest you can't see it between the lines, let me tell you, I truly cared for this lady. A twenty-year relationship develops ties both ways. God took my unprofessional thoughts and bridged a gap to healing for this lady ... and me.

For, as I finished confessing my defective thought pattern, I was led to explore where she was. I asked her if she saw the way the world of medicine approached her as being ineffective. I asked her if she felt like the dam and all that was being done was the next hole was being plugged by the next counseling session or the next medicine. Finally, I asked, "You know I'm waiting for 10 or 15 years to go by and retire. Are you waiting for 20 or 30 years to go by, to die and be done with it all?" Her tears gave the answer before her mouth said, "Yes."

Since that day years ago, I have posed my situation and theirs to many more patients who have had similar journeys as this lady's. It's not a scientific study, yet so far the answer has always been, "Yes." Every one of them! 100% have given up at some level on there being such a thing as a "dam fixer."

Leaking Dam Reality

It seems strange to me. We expect to be able to put men on the Moon and robots on Mars and do it. We expect that when cancer develops, we will find a cure. If we get an infection, we expect to be freed from it. Yet, we just seem to accept that life is a series of ups and downs and our peace and joy will follow those ups and downs. We tend to live life in avoidance and "numb it up pattern" rather than a life filled with eager anticipation of the ups as well as the downs.

Here's an Ol' country doc's test method: If the treatment isn't working, something is wrong. Ask more questions. Is it the wrong treatment, medicine, therapy, dosage, application? Is it the wrong diagnosis? Is it just treating symptoms and not the primary cause? It's time to do some dam fixing!

Healthy Spirit

The spirit side of man needs to be taken care of and addressed if it is to be healthy and move into a life of the "D" of deployment. Just as ignoring your body by not exercising or by over eating leads to body pathology, ignoring the spirit component and not having it as the "sinus node" of your existence will have consequences.

The answer to how to have a healthy spirit is found in John 15 and 16. I have no delusions that I could add anymore to what Jesus lays out there. I simply testify to part of my journey. The pipeline of spiritual fellowship with God has been open wide and flowing when I live out a life of PAUSE, EXAMINE YOUR MOTIVES, ASK as discussed in Chapter 2. I am in over my head. Reminding myself of that while pausing to understand God as able and faithful is a powerful first step in abiding. Acknowledging my sin strengthens my fellowship with Him. Then I just talk to Him, I ask.

Then I wait. I move on living life, because life keeps happening. Sometimes the wait is short and sometimes it's long. Sometimes the answer is what I expected, most of the time it's not. He knows what's best for me. Trusting God, even in the pain.

There are many pragmatic spiritual healthy activities; most people are aware of these. Most people are aware they should exercise and eat correctly, yet they don't. The human capacity to **not** connect the dots is amazing. I really have to fight off a sarcastic spirit when a 53 year-old 389-pound non-exercising man comes into the office and wants me to find out why his knees hurt.

Here are some spirit health activities: Read the Bible daily; memorize verses that are meaningful to you; get in a small group (more on this later); pray; help others/serve; tithe, give generously ...

In the world of medicine we would refer to all the above as health maintenance or preventive medicine. What if there is already some spiritual dysfunction? That leads to the difficulty of first making the right diagnosis and then implementing the correct "treatment."

Spiritual Diagnosis/Treatment

Radio minister Steve Brown says it best, "If it smells like smoke, it must be from the gates of Hell." Making the correct diagnosis of spiritual problems often involves just smelling. Does it "smell" dark? Does it "smell" evil? Does it "smell" like something that makes you want to run and go take a bath or get fresh air? Maybe there is some hard spiritual warfare going on.

Have you tried years of counseling with little return? Are you on the 30th version of an anti-depressant and/or anti-anxiety prescription? Maybe the primary spiritual problem hasn't been addressed.

Once more, if it doesn't make sense, ask more questions. To ask go to PAUSE, EXAMINE YOUR MOTIVES, ASK.

In dealing with the patients medically, it is acceptable, at a certain level, to treat a suspected diagnosis and use that response to help diagnostically. The same can be done spiritually. Let me explain:

Maybe you are in a group you ought to take a break from? Take the break. Did your spirit heal? Hmmmmmmm.

Are your readings of certain material/TV viewing/internet surfing creating issues in your life? Fast from them. Did your spirit heal? Hmmmmmm.

Did you start listening to praise music and you felt closer to God? Hmmmmmmm. (They teach this "Hmmmmmmm" thing in medical school, but you can learn it on your own. I bet there's a You Tube instructional video.)

Did you help with the church's weekend community help project and felt less depressed the following week? Hmmmmmmm.

Did you stop watching pornography and felt cleaner, sleep better, and feel less anxious? Hmmmmmm.

The Enemy

The seed of this book was planted years ago when I noticed the overwhelmingly poor outcomes Godly Christians were having when they tried to live the half-truth of Grandma's Verse

(Chapter One). That "verse" served as a gateway for the Enemy to mess with people, first spiritually then in their soul and in their bodies.

John Eldridge in many of his writings refers to the dangers of making false agreements. I am convinced this is the greatest danger to a person's spiritual health. Every agreement we make with a non-Biblical thought, action or motive, makes us vulnerable to the Enemy. This isn't some fictional Hollywood movie we are in. We have an Enemy who

> ..."prowls around like a roaring lion looking for someone to devour" (1 Peter 5:8)

This is reality. Our sin and the sin of those around us open us up to a vulnerability to the Enemy that the Hollywoodized/ Americanized society has become blind to. Not only blind to, but there is even a belittling attitude toward those who speak of it. Practitioners in medicine seldom address this reality. This attitude has even become the norm in religious communities.

There's an old adage in medical school teachings, "If you don't make the right diagnosis, then you won't select the right treatment." There's a sister adage, " If you're not aware that the diagnosis exists, you won't make that diagnosis."

I'm not just talking about our sin here. That is an issue. It should be confessed and dealt with. This is beyond that. It goes to the issue of what did that sin open you up to, what agreements came with that sin, what demonic foothold did it dig out.

The sin we commit must be confessed and repented of if one is to be spiritually healthy. That's understood in the Christian circle. Is it enough? Yes, from the perspective of fellowship with God. When you sinned, you spiritually made a contract with the Enemy. Even though you are still a Christian, at one level of your life, you have subcontracted with someone else other than God about that area of your life. Like any contract, you are bound to it until it is broken/voided. Confession and repenting are the parts that reconnect you with God.

The next step in spiritual health is to renounce that contract. Renouncing the Enemy's foothold created in your life and then filling that foothold with the Holy Spirit completes the process. In 2 Corinthians, Paul is speaking how God was growing Christians or as he puts it, "being transformed into his image with ever-increasing glory, which come from the Lord, who is the Spirit" (2 Corinthians 3:18 NIV). Then he speaks of that transforming and part of that is having "renounced secret and shameful ways" (2 Corinthians 4:2 NIV).

Our sin opens up demonic footholds related to many areas. The following is just a sampling: lordship, rejection, purity, shame, addiction, abuse, fear, depression, anxiety, egotism, greed, hoarding, discontent, selfish ambition, low self esteem, discouragement, hopelessness, eating disorders, self pity, security issues, insomnia, sorrow, pornography, guilt, workaholism and self-hatred.

Do you ever wonder why there are so many sins we keep repeating, i.e. why we have a chronic spirit illness? The reasons are usually numerous. The consideration should be given to the spiritual warfare the Bible speaks of. Maybe it's time to not address it as the world does (2 Corinthians 10:5-6) and realize what we are really battling (Ephesians 6:12).

I've written of making a "contract" with the Enemy. Another way to view this contract is as a subleasing contract. These spiritual agreements/contracts are like a home (ourselves) that has been bought by a new owner (Christ) and then a basement apartment of the house has been subleased. We shouldn't be surprised when the subleasing Hellion brings in all his smelly offensive stuff. We gave the Enemy permission. He needs to be evicted!

Renouncing the demonic spirits that gained footholds in our life and breaking the contracts by confession of sin will bring the transformation spoken of by Paul. It creates an "ever increasing glory" with the Holy Spirit filling in those areas (Matthew 12:43-45 and Galatians 5:16). That's when we have a healthy spirit and move into a life of the "D" of deployment.

Discharge Plan

Self Examination:

- What area of your life do you have repeated struggles in?

- Where is there hopelessness in your life?

- In the areas you struggle with in your life, do you consider the spiritual realm as a player? Why/Why not?

- Recall a time when you kept fighting the same battles because you failed to see the spirit content as the main problem.

- What area of your life "smells like smoke from the gates of hell"? How are you addressing that area?

- Recall a time when you treated the spiritual component and saw a resolution in the issues in your life.

- Where have you given the Enemy an area to "rent" in your spirit?

- Why does it seem so hard to evict him?

Treatment:

- Take some extra time alone and go make a list of areas where you have spiritual "contracts" with the Enemy. Confess this and ask God's forgiveness. Verbally evict the Enemy.

Rehab:

> "So I say, walk by the Spirit, and you will not gratify the desires of the flesh" (Galatians 5:16)

> "Even When It Hurts" by Hillsong. *Of Dirt and Grace*. Hillsong Music Publishing (APRA) 2015

CHAPTER EIGHT

Body and Soul

"And Jesus grew in wisdom and stature and in
favor with God and Man" (Luke 2:52)

Life is hard.

Life is harder if you're out of shape.

Doctor Google is amazing. Dr. Google is what my staff named the information that my patients find on the Internet. It has helped many of my patients come to an understanding of what is medically happening with them. I've had patients bring in Google-obtained information that was spot on with what was going on with them. Dr. Google does have a greater brain capacity and better recall than I do. More often than not, I am appreciative of Dr. Google. Yet, there's a lot of less-than-accurate information on the internet.

Earlier in this book, I seemed to have been a little harsh to the Grandmas of the world. As I move into this section, I realize how much some of it is going to sound like grandmotherly advice. When it comes to staying healthy, Grandma has the foundational stuff correct: eat right, exercise, get plenty of rest, keep learning, and go to church on Sunday. Let's dig a little deeper in how to "stay healthy" by looking at the next two components we are made of.

Body

When examining a patient, my pattern is to check lung sounds first by listening to the patient's back. I instruct them to breath in and out slowly. Then I move to the front of the chest where my focus turns to listening to the heart. At that point, I usually let the patient know they may breath normally. My patients have often been through this process numerous times and they have learned my pattern. On occasion, as I shift to the heart exam, I will not give the "breath normal" transition command. Often, a long time patient will ask, "Do you want me to keep breathing?" Ahhhh, another "cue line." I love to pause what I'm doing, lift the stethoscope off their chest and say something along the lines of, "If you don't keep breathing you're gonna really mess up my schedule."

Treatment options for the body may seem as obvious as "keep breathing." Yet, it's amazing how we can come up with various ways to mistreat our body and to not take care of it. This would be a good time to reintroduce a mantra that we spoke of earlier and which I hope you will implement: PAUSE, EXAMINE YOUR MOTIVES, ASK. This mantra is about us abiding as a whole, not just our spiritual component.

Most of us have tried to live healthier lives over and over. And, we have failed, over and over. Could it be that the approach we failed with so many times doesn't work because it's the wrong approach? We have made attempts based on a derivative of Grandma's Verse. Most think, "I don't need to bring my health before the Lord because I can handle this." How's that working for you? From here on out when you see "PAUSE, EXAMINE OUR MOTIVES, ASK," take that as an encouragement to remember the lesson from Chapter 2. Let God do a God-work in your life.

In honor of our Grandmas let's begin looking at pragmatic health steps by following her tried and true outline: eat right, exercise, and get plenty of rest. At last count, there were 1,343,612 books on eating correctly. I really will keep this one simple: First: moderation; Second: moderation; Third: moderation. In a general sense, there is no unhealthy food. What tends to make a certain food item unhealthy is how much we eat per meal, how frequent we eat that food item, and what are we not eating that might be healthier. When faced with an eating opportunity: PAUSE, EXAMINE YOUR MOTIVE, ASK.

Let's move on to exercise: Do it. Do it by starting low, go slow. You don't want to hurt yourself.

The story is told of a minister who over a period of years would invite a young man to come to church. The young man would always say that he'd be there that Sunday, then never show. Finally one day after being invited again the young man paused and spoke to the preacher, " I'm gonna tell you why I don't show up." At this the preacher became excited, anticipating how he would counter any issue the young man brought up. The young man said, "Preacher, I can't come because I don't have any mayonnaise." The preacher was so caught off guard and surprised that all he could exclaim was, "What does having mayonnaise have to do with coming to church?"

"Nothing," replied the prospect, "but I figure one excuse is as good as another."

There isn't enough ink and paper to counter, "Why I didn't exercise last night" excuses. Just start moving: PAUSE, EXAMINE YOUR MOTIVES, ASK.

The average adult needs 6 – 8 hours of sleep. Lack of sleep has many contributors. Lack of sleep is more often a symptom of other battles being fought. Check with you doctor. You may need a sleep study to help find the issue. In the meantime, invite God to move in this area: PAUSE, EXAMINE YOU MOTIVES, ASK.

The classic saying goes, "Don't drink, smoke or chew." (Meaning don't drink alcohol, smoke or chew tobacco.) I guess I must have manifestations of a liberal Grandmother and feel the general theme should be moderation if possible, avoidance if needed: PAUSE, EXAMINE YOUR MOTIVES, ASK. When I'm speaking to a smoker, I've been known to half jokingly tell them, "Let's not think of it as stopping, let's just take a break until you're 83 years old. Then you can start back." I figure an 83-year-old can take their own chances of dying younger than if they hadn't smoked.

Spend less time on the media, internet and television. These are just as addictive as alcohol, heroine, hydrocodon. PAUSE, EXAMINE YOUR MOTIVES, ASK.

Using Medicine

Use medicine that your doctor feels appropriate and as instructed. I find it interesting the bias against medicine found in many Christian communities. For the most part, those same people have no trouble going to an orthopedist to fix a broken arm or a surgeon to remove an ill appendix. I respect the concern of how doctors are very quick to just prescribe meds.

It's a real problem. People have car wrecks everyday and I still get in my car to go get a gallon of milk.

This will mess with some of you. Jesus was known to use medicine on people to heal them. Yep, it's true! We spoke of it earlier when we introduced his abiding with his Father. It was there in the healing of the blind man in which he used mud to heal with. That mud was "things" of earth/created material used to bring about healing. By my definition, that is medicine. That is such a critical story. It serves as an encouragement for us to PAUSE, EXAMINE YOUR MOTIVES, ASK when dealing with the area of medicine use. I will be as bold to say, if you're using medicine without asking God about it, you may be handling things on your own. I don't think you want to do that. But, if you don't use medicine without asking God about not using medicine, you may be handling things on your own. I don't think you want to do that either.

A number of my trusted pastor friends consider Jesus' use of mud as medicine a weak example. In 1 Timothy, we find a clearer picture. Paul is writing here to his apprentice, Timothy.

> "Stop drinking only water and use a little wine because of your stomach and your frequent illnesses" (1 Timothy 5:23)

I grew up in a Southern Baptist Church and I can't recall that verse ever being preached on! What's going on here? It doesn't make sense. Ask more questions. Some people have said that Timothy had to use the wine because the water was of poor quality. However, he wasn't told to stop drinking the water. He was instructed to stop drinking water "only." Timothy obviously had frequent illnesses and it is inferred that his stomach was involved. The "medicine" Paul prescribed was wine. From that it is easy to figure out what Timothy's stomach problem was. It wasn't worms as some conjecture. Wine won't cure worms. It wasn't ulcers. Wine is no help with ulcers. Timothy most likely suffered from what Grandma called a "nervous stomach." Today we might put him in the category of Irritable Bowl Syndrome. Timothy was apparently a high intensity fellow and that intensity played havoc with his GI tract. From the therapeutic stand point, that's the only stomach illness wine can help.

There is another challenge here. Why didn't Paul give a more "spiritual" treatment option? Why not pray for healing? Why not have the deacons and elders lay hands on Timothy and "claim" his healing? Why not cast out the spirit of illness in his stomach? If Timothy was so intense and his stomach revealed on occasion that he needed a break, why didn't Paul suggest a sabbatical for the young man? Why not suggest outsourcing some of Timothy's responsibilities? Why not bring in a team of people to help him? Why not suggest that he skip leading that Sunday school class? Instead, Paul essentially says, "Take your medicine." Paul was in an abiding relationship with the Father when he wrote 1 Timothy. He at some level went through PAUSE, EXAMINE YOUR MOTIVES, ASK and what the Father had told him was to tell Timothy to take his medicine. Taking the medicine in light of this *was* a "spiritual" treatment option. Taking care of our body/physical component should be viewed just as spiritual as when we address the soul and spirit components of our nature.

Soul Treatment

The soul (mind/will/emotion) part of humans is remarkable in its diversity and ability to adapt to life changes. It takes data from years of experience and from current situations to formulate plans on how to respond to its current environment. There are two great "diseases" of the soul: misinformation and isolation.

When I was young, the term brainwashing was used to describe various techniques to take an individual and repackage older belief systems while replacing it with a new belief system. The fact that the mind/will/emotion can be affected in this way is both an asset and a liability. Many leaders have used brainwashing as a means to train followers. It can be used to create movements of great achievement or for great destruction.

The brainwashing term has significant negative connotations as does its newer euphemism, indoctrination. A more positive linked term is socialization. These terms acknowledge the seemingly contradictory fact that humans have the ability to learn and also the capacity to deny learning. We also have the ability to remember some things for years and forget other things in minutes.

If two of the greatest enemies of a healthy soul are misinformation and isolation, then to stay soul-healthy or repair a dysfunctional soul it would be wise to learn truth and be around healthy (spiritually speaking) people. It must be noted that some of the things said about keeping a healthy spirit are also said about keeping a healthy soul (mind/will/emotions). This shouldn't come as a surprise since we are all familiar with the effects on our mind/will/emotion if our body doesn't get enough sleep or is ill with a fever virus.

Reading, memorizing and meditating on the Bible is foundational to a healthy soul. For in it are the words of life. Here again, PAUSE, EXAMINE YOUR MOTIVES, ASK provides a clear abiding path to let the Holy Spirit guide you.

The Bible is replete with examples of mentoring relationships. To find a mentor is one of life's wisest decisions. Finding a mentor should be well thought out, prayed about and prioritized. It will not happen by accident. It is a sad commentary on the current state of our society that mentoring is so rare. I'm not sure of the reasons. I conjecture we are too busy or lazy or private or that we undervalue the process. If you are not able to establish such a real life mentor, I suggest tons of reading. I have been "mentored" by the greats such as C.S. Lewis and R.T. Kendall. I have jogged thousands of hours listening to James Dobson, R.C. Sproul, John Maxwell, John Eldridge, Chris Hodges, Harry Reeder, Craig Groeschel and Henry Blackerby via their audio recordings. I consider these men my mentors due to the time I put in learning from them.

Counseling for Christians is often as controversial as Christians using prescription medicine. The argument goes that as Christians we already are connected to the Great Counselor. Though this is the reassuring encouragement from Jesus in John 16, there is nothing scripturally spoken against Christians receiving counseling. It would be within reason to only be counseled by a Christian counselor. It seems that psychologists, life coaches and trained counselors are filling in the gap for the missing mentors. I have been known to refer to them as "mercenary mentors." I don't mean to be derogatory. I find that many patients receive well the idea of going to a counselor if it's packaged as being mentored.

Small groups of fellow strugglers are where change takes place. I'm not talking "warm fuzzy talk about the weather and the sports score last night" group. Those have a place. But, it's rare for real growth and healing to be there. No, the type of group I'm talking about is the "warts showin', tears flowin' and every now and then somebody says truth to you in such a way that in spite of it steppin' all over your toes you want to hug 'em" kinda group. If your group isn't headed that way, find another one. Keep looking until you do find one. If you can't find one, START ONE!

And, here is where you will find the potential for being the healthiest soul, when we are leading others. In the position of being the leader your desperation for God grows. In this role God will redeem your past misery and mistakes of your life as you share of God's wonderful grace and mercy given to you and available to your group members. Big letter time!

YOU WERE NEVER INTENDED TO NEVER MENTOR SOMEONE.

Or, to say it another way, you are intended to mentor someone. Matthew 28:18-20 is known as the "Great Commission." In those verses, Jesus is declaring our obligation to go tell of him. Part of that is mentoring. Mentoring others makes you seek true information and mentoring can't be done in isolation. The result is a healthy soul.

Discharge Plan

Self Examination:

- What excuses do you have for why you don't:
    - start moving more
    - eat smaller servings
    - consume less unhealthy stuff
    - have fewer electronic devices consuming your day
    - join a small group
    - memorize scripture
    - lead others
- What barriers are in your life that needs removing to see a breakthrough in the above areas?
- What area of your soul and body do you struggle with most often? Why?
- What medicine are you taking/not taking without abiding in PAUSE, EXAMINE YOUR MOTIVES AND ASKING God about?
- What counseling are you in/not in without abiding in PAUSE, EXAMINE YOUR MOTIVES AND ASKING God about?
- Why do you avoid challenging/hard small group studies?
- What keeps you from finding a mentor?
- What keeps you from being a mentor?

Treatment:

- Change things in your life ... your bed time ... sitting time ... TV time ... reading time ... small group involvement ... your role in your small group ...

Rehab:

"Blessed is the one who does not walk in step with the wicked or stand in the way that sinners take or sit in the company of mockers, but whose delight is in the law of the Lord, and who meditates on his law day and night. That person is like a tree planted by streams of water, which yields its fruit in season and whose leaf does not wither—whatever they do prospers" (Psalm 1:1-3)

"Healer" by Kari Jobe. *Kari Jobe*. Integrity Music. 2009.

CHAPTER NINE

Facing the Unexpected

"And we rejoice in the hope of the glory of God. Not only so, but we also rejoice in our sufferings because we know that suffering produces perseverance, perseverance, character, and character hope" (Romans 5: 2-4)

Life is hard.

Life is harder if you don't embrace the blessings in the overwhelmingly unexpected.

World War II demonstrated different approaches in distributing leadership and decision-making responsibilities. The war was fought between what was termed the Axis and Allied powers. Germany was part of the Axis coalition. Its headquarters were in Berlin. The leadership in Berlin was very "hands on" in the day-to-day, field-to-field battle decisions. It was not unusual for a German commander in France to have to wait hours to get approval to move several dozen tanks a few miles to gain an advantage on his adversary.

The Allies, on the other hand, gave its field commanders more leeway in achieving their overall desired objective. Thus, an Allied leader on the actual field of battle could gather data quickly, see changes that could be made at that time, implement those changes and win a battle.

Many historians feel these different approaches caused the Axis to lose the war. The goal of this book is to provide guiding principles as we face life's battles. The goal is not to address every particular type of hardship in life, because many will be unexpected and unique.

Life Battles With Others

My thought patterns of life were developed in the land of Forrest Gump. I find simple word pictures are all I can often grasp. When I was younger, I pictured addressing people and challenging situations as a seesaw activity.

One side of the seesaw was occupied by the opportunity to apply mercy and grace to the situations or people. On the other side sat accountability and consequences. The seesaw was balanced upon the fulcrum called love. The simple idea seemed to be to balance mercy/grace with accountability/consequences on the love I had from God for those situations and people.

MERCY   **CONSEQUENCES**
GRACE   **ACCOUNTABILITY**

LOVE

Life is more complicated than that. It became apparent that each side of the seesaw could be applied with different motives behind that application. Those motives fell into one of two categories: negative motives or positive motives. Here are a few examples first.

The wife of an alcoholic man may be asked by that man to call his boss one Monday morning to tell the boss he won't be at work that day because he is ill. Well, the man is sort of ill, if a hangover counts as an illness. Though she's frustrated with her husband, if she lets him suffer the consequences, then her spouse may be fired and this fills her with fear. Fear is a negative motivation. She uses this negative motivation to apply grace/mercy on the situation and calls the boss. The drinking will continue.

Another example: A teenage girl has displayed an arrogant "know it all" attitude one too many times to her dad. Her dad has developed a bitter attitude (negative motivation) in this area toward his daughter. One day, as she leaves for school, he sees her gym clothes left on the couch. His bitterness gives him pleasure in applying accountability/consequences as he contemplates her having to sit in the bleachers during gym time. His bitterness progressed into vengefulness.

One last example: A young boy had broken a house rule one more time. It was one of those rules that was put in place to protect from great physical harm. He knew the punishment for breaking such a rule with such grave consequences was a firm swat on the bottom with a wooden kitchen spoon. Having been caught and convicted (by Mom), they were now in the kitchen ready for the spoon of justice to be applied. Under a hope-filled desire (positive motive) for her son to understand Jesus taking our punishment on the cross, she swung the spoon and struck herself. She then proceeded to share why she took his punishment. He never broke that rule again.

Mercy/grace and accountability/consequences in and of themselves are morally neutral. It's like money. Money is morally neutral. It can be used for the purpose of good or evil. In a similar way mercy/grace and accountability/consequences can be used to bring about purposes that serve for good or evil.

Mercy/grace applied with fear - hopelessness, guilt, coercion, confusion, passive aggressiveness - in order to manipulate will have outcomes found in the land of discipline and development. Mercy/grace applied as God directs with faith, protection, sacrifice, hope ... will be blessed with deployment adventures and the peace that come with it.

Accountability/consequences applied with bitterness, vengefulness, exasperation, frustration, Godless anger, etc., will have outcomes found in the land of discipline and development. Accountability/consequences applied as God directs with conviction, hope, clear communication, maintaining integrity, concern, thoughtfulness, respecting the law, and so forth, will be blessed with deployment adventures and the peace that come with it.

The key to Godly success in this area is that little phrase, "as God directs." Each and every decision should be done while in an abiding position as is found in our old friend PAUSE, EXAMINE YOUR MOVTIVE, ASK. The scriptural reassurance is found that if we ask while abiding, He will answer. The choice between mercy/grace and accountability/consequences is one in which God should take the lead.

By "blessed," I don't necessarily mean it will feel easy or smooth. Nor do I mean it will be painless. Nor does it mean you won't be harassed, second guessed, ridiculed, betrayed, verbally abused, doubted, falsely accused, shunned, misunderstood, isolated, ostracized, hated, detested or physically imperiled. The external worldly consequences are not the litmus test for blessing. I would like to say that internally there would always be a peace about the choices. Granting that peace is God's prerogative and I have found that sometimes it comes later. I'm just to do the next "right" thing. That "right" thing is to do the will of the Father.

Jesus Failed

Jesus failed. Well, by the standard of most of the people I have challenged with the following take on a familiar event from the Bible.

Mark 10:17-22 shares the story that is often referred to as the encounter with the rich, young ruler. The scene: Jesus is with his disciples teaching them of God when a man interrupts class. The man has a powerful question for Jesus. He is so humbly desperate that he falls on his knees before Jesus.

> "As Jesus started on his way, a man ran up to him and fell on his knees before him. 'Good teacher,' he asked, 'what must I do to inherit eternal life?'
>
> 'Why do you call me good?' Jesus answered. 'No one is good – except God alone. You know the commandments: 'You shall not murder, you shall not commit adultery, you shall not steal, you shall not give false testimony, you shall not defraud, honor your father and mother.' '
>
> 'Teacher,' he declared, 'all these I have kept since I was a boy'" (Mark 10:17-20)

Verse 21 shares something Jesus did that isn't spoken so directly of any other person in the Bible. He looked at him and loved him.

"Jesus looked at him and loved him. 'One thing you lack,' he said. 'Go, sell everything you have and give to the poor, and you will have treasure in heaven. Then come, follow me.' At this the man's face fell. He went away sad, because he had great wealth" (Mark 10:21-22)

The young man gets up, turns and walks away. The total interaction seems to have taken less than 45 seconds.

There used to be an encouraging bracelet campaign called "What Would Jesus Do?" ("WWJD" was what was printed on the rubber bracelets.) The idea was to face any situation you were in by addressing it with the question, "What would Jesus do?"

Let's play a variation on that question: This time we will try "WWIDAJIIWRITSS" (What Would I Do As Jesus If I Were Really In That Same Situation). Yes, that might be a large bracelet. Let's have you stand in for Jesus in the events of Mark 10. You've looked at this humble seeker and you love him. Love means you want what's best for him. You give him a succinct and clear answer, THE correct answer for that man. There is no hostility in this moment. Only love. Then he turns and walks away from you. What would you do at that moment? Be very real in your response to the question. Be brutally honest. Don't give some hyper-spiritual, pretend, well-thought-out response. Put your self there, in that 45-second encounter. The man is walking away without another word. You may never see him again. You love him. What would you **REALLY** do?

Here's what most of us would do: Chase after the guy! Chase after him and say something like, "Hey, wait! Let me clarify." Or,

"Hey, can we talk later. I'm free for breakfast on Thursday." Or, "Hey, sorry I was so short with the answer. These twelve slow-learning guys have got me worn down." (Those of you who say you'd answer otherwise, you either didn't need this book to begin with or you are as cold as ice or, sadly, you would lie!)

Since most of us would have done it differently than Jesus, it's fair to say we feel Jesus failed. He failed to handle this situation correctly according to "WWIDASIIWRITSS."

Jesus just let him walk away. Why? Remember, Jesus only did what his Father told him. We therefore know God wanted Jesus to let the ruler leave and for class to resume. Jesus wasn't a failure. He was abiding with the Father.

Can you imagine the disdain toward Jesus by some who saw this? Contemplate the second-guessing that was going on by those who were in the crowd. Envision the guilt some would try to load on Jesus because he "failed."

Jesus didn't fail. He did the "right" thing by doing the will of the Father. Jesus followed the Father's lead and left the consequences up to the Father as Jesus moved in deployment (he dwelt continually in this "D") sharing how life is lived with the Father.

An Improved Word Picture

I used the mercy/grace accountability/consequences seesaw word picture for years. Though I found it very useful, there was something about it that felt very disconcerting and rather hopeless. It seemed so static. It seemed purposeless. It gave me the feeling I get when people describe the yen-yang approach of just finding balance in life.

The Coosa River begins near Rome, Georgia, and winds 280 miles through valleys of the Appalachian foothills into middle Alabama. Before the days of the United States, it was home to many Cherokee and Creek Indians. During the last 100 years, many man-made dams have tamed the river. One of those dams forms Lay Lake. I am blessed to have in-laws who have a log cabin on that lake.

Lay Lake is home to a growing number of Bald Eagles. I've been there enough to become somewhat familiar with their flight patterns and a few of their favorite fishing spots. It was while watching these beautiful creatures that my seesaw word picture discomfort was solved. God used a windy day, my word picture failure, a famous Bible verse and an eagle to bring peace to me about God using hard times in our lives.

To fly, the eagle uses a combination of its own wing flapping, wind and what is referred to as thermals. Thermals, according to Dr. Google, are the updraft in a small-scale convective current, i.e. air moving up. For most of its flying time, the eagle will not have to flap its wings. This is especially true of the times it is soaring.

Here's our famous verse:

> "... but those who hope in the Lord will renew their strength. They will soar on wings like eagles; they will run and not grow weary, they will walk and not be faint" (Isaiah 40:31)

While watching one of my eagle friends one windy day, I noticed how effortlessly he moved about. This was not true of the local Great Heron. The heron had fought and stumbled his way through the heavy breeze and hid in a slew. The crows stayed aloft longer than the heron; The crow's efforts, however, were associated with tremendous flapping of wings and an erratic flight pattern determined more by wind directions than its muscular endeavors.

But, the eagle - oh the eagle - effortlessly, so incredibly effortlessly, moved smoothly through the seemingly overwhelming wind. It not only conquered the wind, it was using it to further the raptor's own adventure. If the desire were to go one direction, a mere application change in wing angle or pitch accomplished the task. Seeking to go another route, adjustments made in the other wing would bring that about. And, occasionally it would set its wings in a fixed position and up it soared and soared and soared ... without effort. It could do this if at any point it was tired and needed to regain strength. Hence, there's truth in the wording of the verse. Yes, an eagle can renew its strength while soaring in the midst of windy opposition.

If an eagle were to be viewed head-on in flight, its overall pattern would be that of a seesaw: a horizontal "beam" (its wings) over a centrally located fulcrum (its body). I was close with the seesaw word picture, however it failed to work. God didn't use a seesaw word picture. He used an eagle. He doesn't expect our lives to be played out in a fixed location trying to find balance. We are meant to be headed somewhere. That journey will have its ups and downs. There will be missions to accomplish. There will be storms and wind.

To accomplish our missions, we will need to follow His leading, applying grace/mercy when He instructs. When He directs, we need to put a little downward force on the wing of accountability/consequences. At other times, we will lift the wing of grace and mercy to take us in the direction He wants us to go. Trust God's leading in the times of pain, disappointment, grief, betrayal, job loss and financial crisis. God didn't instruct us to handle the hard times on our own. With Him, we're to USE the hard times like the eagle uses the overwhelming unexpected wind. USE the hard times because until we get to heaven, life is hard.

Discharge Plan

Self Examination:

- Do you have an aversion or propensity to apply grace/mercy over accountability/consequences or accountability/consequences over grace/mercy?

- Recall a time when you used negative motivation to apply grace/mercy or accountability/consequences.

- Recall a time when you followed God's leading in applying mercy/grace or accountability/consequences even when you didn't really feel like it.

- Do you look at people's responses to determine if you made the "right" choices in life?

- Do you look to preconceived expected results of your actions to determine if you made the "right" choices in life?

Treatment:

- Practice checking your motives behind the times when you apply grace/mercy or accountability/consequences.
- Seek God's leading in applying grace/mercy or accountability/consequences.

Rehab:

> "... but those who hope in the LORD will renew their strength. They will soar on wings like eagles; they will run and not grow weary, they will walk and not be faint" (Isaiah 40:31)

> "Blessings" by Laura Story. *Blessings.* INO Records. 2011

CHAPTER TEN

Soaring in the Storm

"You intended to harm me, but God intended it for good to accomplish what is now being done, the saving of many lives" (Genesis 50:20)

Life is hard.

Life is harder than expected, and that's not a "bad" thing.

Remembering people's names has always been a challenge for me. I think subconsciously it is one of the reasons I chose the career I did. The person in front of me usually is the one whose name is written on the chart in my hand.

Sundays are when my brain is most likely to be in shutdown mode. This is especially true on Sunday evenings. It is even more so true Sunday evenings when I roll the garbage out to the street for Monday garbage pick-up. It's a very mindless job. It was at that particular time a few years back when the message of this book became very real and personal to me.

My brother and his wife have raised four girls. Two have moved to Miami. One lives with her husband in North Carolina where they have an ever-growing family. I sometimes refer to her as the "baby-birthing machine." The last daughter is single and is a gifted musician who manages a local restaurant.

On that particular Sunday night, I was cluelessly strolling the week's waste to the side of the curb when my cell phone rang. Looking at the caller ID I noticed it was one of my niece's phone number.

"Hello!"

"Hey Uncle Doug, this is 'K.'"

"What's up?" I inquired.

"Well, I'm calling to let you know I'm pregnant."

"Well, that's great!" These words seemed appropriate because I knew that the "baby-birthing machine" wanted to have lots of babies.

Yet, the quietness and slightly hesitant response from my niece planted the seed in my mind that something was amiss. As she spoke of the other family members responses, I became aware of a possible explanation. Checking my caller ID again, I confirmed my thoughts. The niece I was speaking with was not the "baby-birthing machine," it was the unmarried niece!

Then I replayed my words in my mind, "Well, that's great!"

Sometimes the mind can move awfully fast as the rest of the world moves slowly. My first thought was, "Doug, you've done it again. You confused somebody's name." Then I thought about telling her of my error and explaining my comments. I'd like to say I had really pure Christ-like thoughts, but I didn't. My hyper-accelerated thoughts were going a different direction: You're an idiot and you're gonna look like an idiot to her.

Then I pondered where I would go with my explaining the name confusion. I would first have to tell her the error I'd made. Then came the thought that really messed with me. Telling her of my error would also lead me down the road to having to retract my "Well, that's great!" verbiage. Meaning, I would at some level have to tell her what she already knew, and was hearing from others, "this isn't great!"

My warp-speed thinking then took me to what I knew from my personal experience and job as a physician. I knew of many, many people who had been where my niece was and was going. By in-large and for the most part, everyone of them experienced some wonderful aspect of life and God's love as a result of their out-of-wedlock experience.

As I said, some of my multiple motives were less than commendable. But, I felt very led to continue my speech down the road where my first bumbling had led me.

I then spoke words that were not my own. For, quite honestly, I didn't fully believe them myself at that moment. I decided to trust God. I told her it was going to be fine. I told her that God was going to be with her. I said it would be hard. I told her we'd pray for her. I told her to let me know what she needed. I'd be there for her.

That pregnancy produced a wonderful boy who has brought much love into the extended Moore family. Until she saw the rough draft for this chapter, I had not shared the above with my niece. Maybe I still am losing a battlefield of pride. In the years since this occurrence, I have been very well-treated at any restaurant my niece manages.

Answered Prayer

I now have a more challenging time when I hear petitions being made for prayer requests. Where as before, whatever I was asked to pray, I prayed. Most times my prayers then were weak and mostly ineffective prayers. Now I find that to be like Christ, I must abide in Him. So, I pause, examine my motives, and ask the Father what He wants.

The story of Joseph's hard life is shared in Genesis 37-41. I imagine that Joseph prayed to God for his brothers to be filled with mercy and pity for him. I can see him praying for his freedom. It's not farfetched to envision him praying for a witness to testify for him after his boss's wife framed him. He surely prayed that he would be freed quickly from jail. It seems that we often see the following as what played out in the heavenly realm regarding Joseph.

God is in heaven doing his "God stuff." A distressed angel appears before him and reports that Joseph, the very one God gave a dream about future rulership, has been sold as a slave by his brothers. God springs into action and immediately checks into all his plan " B" options. One option is to have the slave traders sell him into the home of a man who is a high-ranking Egyptian politico. The potential dream destruction by Joseph's brothers has been thwarted.

In the course of time, the poor angel has to return and report another obstacle has appeared. Joseph's boss's wife has framed him for rape. Again, God checks into all his options and gets Joseph's life spared and puts him in jail with some of the ruler's officials. And, so we seem to see God moving from Plan A to Plan B to Plan C to Plan D.

If I were given permission to make a movie of what my Holy imagination would do with the Genesis story of Joseph, here is what some of the script would look like:

God:
"Angels come here and watch this. See that guy there?"

Angel #1:
"Yes, that's Joseph. He's the guy you gave the dream to about his future as a ruler.

God:
"That's right. And, I have a protective hedge about his life. Watch what happens when I lower that protection a little."

Angel #2:
"Oh my God!" (He can get by with saying this since he is talking to God.) "His brothers sold him into slavery!"

God:
"Yes, I knew the brothers' envy would lead them to do that. Watch what I'm about to do."

Angel #1:
"Oh wow! You had him sold to one of Pharaoh's main officials. You've moved him closer to a position of ruling."

God:
"Yeah. Now, see what happens if I drop my protection again."

Angel #3:
"That woman just lied about Joseph and framed him!"

God:
"Yep. Yet, I've got him. I knew her desire for him would lead her to such betrayal. Look at this."

Angel #2
"You helped him encourage a friend. Yet, you haven't helped the friend remember Joseph."

God:
"Oh, I will help his friend remember. It will be at the time most helpful for Joseph."

This scene is consistent with the words of encouragement Joseph gave his brothers regarding their actions.

"You intended to harm me, but God intended it
for good to accomplish what is now being done,
the saving of many lives" (Genesis 50:20)

God has demonstrated his willingness to send hard times in the lives of those He loves to accomplish His purpose. How can I know how to pray? The times and events are from God. It would seem wise to ask Him how He'd have me pray.

"... You do not have because you do not ask God" (James 4:2)

Compromised Days in God's Hands

Here's something that will mess with you. In my own conservative Judeo Christian approach, I would probably have handled Jesus' mother's situation poorly. Look at the state of the society at Mary's time. The government was very secular and non-Biblical. The religious leaders were caught up in their concerns over religious minutia. Yet, these same leaders forgot to adhere to Torah's instructions to stone an adulteress. That would have "clearly" included Mary.

I'm not sure when the rules were first compromised. Maybe the head priest favorite cousin's daughter got caught in adultery. He made an exception for her. Then on another occasion, another compromise/exception was made. Pretty soon, nobody is following God's precepts. Roman laws also forbid her stoning. Yet, the Jewish leadership compromised their faith by fearing Rome more than God.

And yet, into these compromised days, God has Mary become pregnant with Jesus. Those very days of compromise, God uses as an opportunity to bring Amazing Grace into our world. The "bad" laxity of religious rulers God uses to save Mary's life. I would probably have been praying to God about how the world was such a mess and needs to be straightened out by getting new leaders. My words might be true. He, however, was up to something bigger.

Paul's View

> "Now I want you to know, brothers and sisters, that what has happened to me has actually served to advance the gospel. As a result, it has become clear throughout the whole palace guard and to everyone else that I am in chains for Christ. And because of my chains, most of the brothers and sisters have become confident in the Lord and dare all the more to proclaim the gospel without fear" (Philippians 1:12-14)

It isn't a stretch of the imagination to come to the conclusion that Paul at some level had PAUSED, EXAMINED HIS MOTIVES, ASKED God for the way to proceed in regards to speaking at the local synagogue. He probably pondered the topic, the verses of scripture to reference, the length of time he would speak, and the tone he would use to address his hearers.

He may have had someone advise for him to move on to the next town. He may have thought that also. I'm sure the Enemy was whispering it in his ears.

Yet, he preached to the people who ultimately threw him in jail. Paul was in the same vein as Joseph during the Potipher's wife temptation episode. They both did the right thing, said the right thing, at the right time and for the right reason (to do God's desire). And, the results for them, time in jail!

He didn't see this as a bad thing. Instead, he sees God moving and using the situation. I wonder if he had visitors in jail telling him how he should have left town, should have chosen a different topic or used a different tone. I fear I might have been one of those. I probably would have expressed what a waste of his speaking talents and skills. Wouldn't it have been better for Paul to be moving from town-to-town sharing Gospel truth? Paul, though, heads on a different route.

Even Paul was a little narrow in his view of what God was doing. He saw God as using him to give testimony to the palace guard and encouragement to Paul's fellow Christians. Don't you know Paul was blown away when he got to heaven to see what God had done with this hard time in prison? The letter Paul had written while there, God has used for about 2,000 years to share the Gospel. God's use of jail time did more than Paul's circuit riding tour ever could have.

The Redeeming of the Permanent

God's road map of life has no dead ends. He is a God of redemption. Our past is our past. It is permanently set in history. Those less than honorable moments, those times of pain, those missed opportunities, those episodes of betrayal, that death, whatever the hardships and troubles, they all have a permanent reality. Yet, there is not finality there. God is into redeeming the permanent. We can't change the past. We err if we live in it (Philippians 3:13). Let God redeem it. As my friend, Jim Kelly, says, "You can't leave a legacy for the future by looking over your shoulder to the past."

Soaring Free: Verses That Will Mean More

Storms of life will come. Ecclesiastes speaks of these times. Chapter 3 presents many elements of this life we live.

> "There is a time for everything, and a season
> for every activity under the heavens:
> a time to be born and a time to die, a time to plant and a
> time to uproot,
> a time to kill and a time to heal, a time to tear down and a
> time to build,
> a time to weep and a time to laugh, a time to mourn and a
> time to dance,
> a time to scatter stones and a time to gather them, a time
> to embrace and a time to refrain from embracing,
> a time to search and a time to give up, a time to keep and
> a time to throw away,
> a time to tear and a time to mend, a time to be silent and
> a time to speak,
> a time to love and a time to hate, a time for war and a
> time for peace" (Ecclesiastes 3:1-8)

In those storms, well meaning-Christians will often speak verses meant to encourage us. Yet, for many, those verses bring anything but encouragement. They seem to be "bumper sticker" verses. By that I mean, they are very familiar to most, yet few people truly own them. In fact, since they are not "real" to the person in the storm, they often become sources of guilt, condemnation and further misery: "I don't feel like the verse speaks to me;" "I must be a failure;" "I'm too spiritually immature;" "I'll never get what the verse says;" It's really meant as a vague goal that we will only achieve in heaven ..."

The two contracts spoken of in Chapter 4 lead to two different responses to scriptures. These scriptures were meant by God to give us hope in the present, in the midst of the storms of life. The Enemy's contract leads to the despairing remarks above. We would do wisely to reject that Godless contract, break its agreement and evict the Enemy.

Embracing the blessings of overwhelmingly unexpected hard times empowers the Holy Spirit to use those times. He uses those times to produce the fruit of the spirit (love, joy, peace, forbearance, kindness, goodness, faithfulness, gentleness and self-control as in Galatians 5:22-23). Consider the implications of any of the Biblical victories in hard times (i.e. David's victory over Goliath; Noah's victory over the flood; the blind man healed by Jesus; the lake storm calmed to save the disciples.) Ponder this: David had to have a Goliath in his life to have the victory; Noah had to have a flood to receive deliverance; the blind man had to be blind to be healed; there had to be a storm to be calmed in order to see the power of Jesus. Understanding God's view of our life's hard time allows the following verses and many more to take on the freedom and power they were designed for.

"Rejoice in the Lord always. I will say it again: Rejoice!" (Philippians 4:4)

... becomes a realistic part of life. If I see God working His good for me, not labeling His work as bad, I will rejoice always. Even in my tears of grief and pain, there will be an element of rejoicing in the Lord. Ponder how these verses become more practical:

"Rejoice always, pray continually, give thanks in all circumstances; for this is God's will for you in Christ Jesus" (1 Thessalonians 5:16-18)

"Keep your lives free from the love of money and be content with what you have, because God has said, "Never will I leave you; never will I forsake you" (Hebrews 13:5)

"And we know that in all things God works for the good of those who love him, who have been called according to his purpose" (Romans 8:28)

"If you say, "The LORD is my refuge," and you make the Most High your dwelling, no harm will overtake you, no disaster will come near your tent" (Psalm 91:9-10)

"... but, whoever listens to me will live in safety and be at ease, without fear of harm" (Proverbs 1:33)

"You will keep in perfect peace those whose minds are steadfast, because they trust in you" (Isaiah 26:3)

"Consider it pure joy, my brothers and sisters, whenever you face trials of many kinds, because you know that the testing of your faith produces perseverance. Let perseverance finish its work so that you may be mature and complete, not lacking anything" (James 1:2-4)

"Therefore I tell you, do not worry about your life, what you will eat or drink; or about your body, what you will wear. Is not life more than food, and the body more than clothes? Look at the birds of the air; they do not sow or reap or store away in barns, and yet your heavenly Father feeds them. Are you not much more valuable than they? Can any one of you by worrying add a single hour to your life? "And why do you worry about clothes? See how the flowers of the field grow. They do not labor or spin. Yet I tell you that not even Solomon in all his splendor was dressed like one of these. If that is how God clothes the grass of the field, which is here today and tomorrow is thrown into the fire, will he not much more clothe you - you of little faith? So do not worry, saying, 'What shall we eat?' or 'What shall we drink?' or 'What shall we wear?' For the pagans run after all these things, and your heavenly Father knows that you need them. But seek first his kingdom and his righteousness, and all these things will be given to you as well. Therefore, do not worry about tomorrow, for tomorrow will worry about itself. Each day has enough trouble of its own" (Matthew 6:25-34)

Life is hard. But, it can be lived with the peace of the martyrs. My job is to do the will of The Father. He will bring the results and He declares His results good. Life is easier if you trust God.

Discharge Plan

Self Examination:

- Why do you find it hard to see God bringing good from your hardship?
- What currently is your hardest battle?
- Recall a time when a hope-filled verse was "useless" to you.
- Why was it "useless?"
- If a verse seems impotent, where should we look for the source of its weakness?
- What permanent part of your past needs redeeming?
- Where in your environment (work, home, society ...) do you find Biblical standards compromised? How can God use you to be his vessel for redemption there?

Treatment:

- Embrace the overwhelmingly unexpected with an understanding of God's redeeming nature.

Rehab:

"And we know that in all things God works for the good of those who love him, who have been called according to his purpose" (Romans 8:28)

"Dear friends, do not be surprised at the fiery ordeal that has come on you to test you, as though something strange were happening to you. But rejoice inasmuch as you participate in the sufferings of Christ, so that you may be overjoyed when his glory is revealed. If you are insulted because of the name of Christ, you are blessed, for the Spirit of glory and of God rests on you. If you suffer, it should not be as a murderer or thief or any other kind of criminal, or even as a meddler. However, if you suffer as a Christian, do not be ashamed, but praise God that you bear that name" (1 Peter 4:12-16)

"Praise be to the God and Father of our Lord Jesus Christ, the Father of compassion and the God of all comfort, who comforts us in all our troubles, so that we can comfort those in any trouble with the comfort we ourselves receive from God. For just as we share abundantly in the sufferings of Christ, so also our comfort abounds through Christ. If we are distressed, it is for your comfort and salvation; if we are comforted, it is for your comfort, which produces in you patient endurance of the same sufferings we suffer. And our hope for you is firm, because we know that just as you share in our sufferings, so also you share in our comfort" (2 Corinthians 1:3-7)

"Not only so, but we also glory in our sufferings, because we know that suffering produces perseverance; perseverance, character; and character, hope. And hope does not put us to shame, because God's love has been poured out into our hearts through the Holy Spirit, who has been given to us" (Romans 5:3-5)

"God Moves in Mysterious Ways" by Jeremy Riddle. *Full Attention*. Varietal Records. 2007.

Epilogue

"Be very careful, then, how you live—not as unwise but as wise, making the most of every opportunity, because the days are evil. Therefore do not be foolish, but understand what the Lord's will is" (Ephesians 5:15-17)

A Goal and a Contrast

If the Lord grants, I will continue to grow old in this hard life.

I have as one of my goals in life to become a pleasant agreeable elderly resident of a nursing home. Yes, it's a strange goal. The way I figure it, we are going to spend eternity in heaven. So, staying here to the max time is really not going to shorten my heavenly experience.

My desire is to live my life in such a way as to be content finishing with all my worldly possession's being in a 12 by 14 foot room. It seems that to have a nice bed, a comfortable chair, and a TV should be enough at that point in life...that and people. For we all need others...others to minister to and to receive ministry from.

I picture myself as a quasi-demented ol' man. One day my grand nephew comes to visit me. He is in the middle of life and he has discovered something. He has discovered that life is hard. He is discovering life is harder if he tries to make square pegs fit into round holes ... if he moves through life not recognizing self imposed unrealities ... if he takes a job that wasn't his ... if he tries to avoid "bad" events ... if he is messed up ... if he keeps making the same mistakes ... if he is out of shape. He has discovered that he is overwhelmed. He is desperate. He is desperate for so many things. More than anything, he is desperate for hope. In his desperation, I come to his mind.

Through the years, he has heard me speak of my life's journey. He, of course, has seen the "broken in" and more experienced Doug Moore. The Doug Moore he has seen is one that "rejoices always," "gives thanks in all circumstances," and (even though a little forgetfully demented) has a "steadfast mind" in regards to life and God. He sees in that nursing home prisoner, a man who has tasted "perfect peace" here on this side of eternity. And so, he seeks me out. He needs to tell someone. He needs someone to hear his pain. He needs someone to confess his shortcomings. He comes to a fellow struggler with whom he feels safe. He also subconsciously comforts himself with the idea that the forgetful geriatric will forget anything any body tells him because the gray-haired guy can't even remember the channel number of ESPN! He'd be right about that last thing. But, the worn out Southerner sitting in the last chair he'll ever own, can recall God declaring life good.

In that small nursing home chamber, my relative will tell me of his current battle. He just got news that he has gotten his girlfriend pregnant. She will lose her college scholarship if she keeps the baby. Finances are already hard and will certainly get harder. He will weep. He will look at an old beat-up doctor for help and wisdom. I hope I will speak thusly:

"Do you love her?"

"Yes."

"Does she love you?"

"Yes."

"Ya gonna marry her?"

"Yes."

"Do y'all love the Lord?"

"Yes ... but I feel like I failed Him."

"He wasn't surprised," I'll softly reply. "Do you still talk to Him?"

"Yes." He'll pause and then speak from deep in his body, soul, and spirit, "I'm overwhelmed!"

"Yep. Keep talking to Him, listening to Him. Welcome to the major leagues of life. Where you are is hard. Where you are going stands to be harder. But, it is gonna be fine. It's gonna be good. I promise."

He won't wholly believe me at that moment. Yet, he will believe at some level in some embryonic way.

I can promise this because it is true.

Contrasting Stories

For years, I've shared the lessons of this book to folks in my practice. I have found they receive it better if I paint a word picture of what an overwhelmed life can look like. I contrast two parallel events. One version lived deeming things "bad." The other version lived deeming things as they are.

The setting of the stories is in a car. The driver is a Christian. The passenger is a non-Christian whom the driver has been speaking with for quite some time. They had met at an outpatient physical therapy office. Both are receiving therapy for recent shoulder surgeries. The Biblical truth's shared have brought changes in the non-Christian's life. The Christian has discerned where his passenger is spiritually and has arranged for the two of them to attend a concert by a contemporary worship group. The driver has heard the words sung and spoken in the concert have been powerfully useful to those at the same spiritual point as his passenger. The night of the concert is stormy as the remnants of a recent tropical storm move over the area. Midway through the drive to the show the car experiences a flat tire. First, we will see what happens when we have a Christian driver who has yet to understand as Christians, we ARE NOT given the

Right

Privilege

Honor

Authority

Position

Command

to ever label an event, occurrence, adventure, episode, or hardship as "bad."

Upon detecting the flat tire our eager Christian exclaims, "Ah man, a flat tire! That's bad; we're not going to get there early! It won't be good if we don't get good seats. Your shoulder and mine aren't well enough to change a tire. At least I have AAA to help."

The call to AAA leads to the driver finding out that it will be 30 minutes before help arrives. Frustrated he bemoans, "Thirty minutes … right! They never get that right. I bet it will be closer to 45 minutes." Then he spends the time until rescue arrival entertaining his traveling friend with past stories of "bad breakdown" adventures.

Meanwhile at the home of the wrecker guy who will help our pair, the wrecker guy's son is experiencing an asthma attack brought on by the weather change. His wife is overwhelmed with the situation. Our poor hero is caught between a cell phone flat tire rescue call, a decompensating wife, and a child he's trying to keep from having a third trip to the ER this year.

Having calmed both the asthma attack and his wife, the exhausted man arrives to help the future concert attendees. It has been 45 minutes since the driver placed the call. The driver boasts, "I told you he'd be late! This situation is going from bad to worse." Then he rolls down the window and shares his frustration with his rescuer.

"You're 15 minutes later than they said you'd be! It's bad enough that we're going to be late. Now you're making us even later!" (I wonder if the tire is changed as fast as it could be changed.) All the while, the passenger is watching, listening and pondering. I wonder what words will be sung and spoken at the concert to undo what he has just lived through?

After sharing this version of the adventure, I contrast it with the adventure of a Christian who deems things as they are.

Upon detecting the flat tire our eager Christian exclaims, "Ah man, a flat tire! That's going to make us late. Your shoulder and mine aren't well enough to change a tire. I have AAA to call and get help."

The call to AAA leads to the driver finding out that it will be 30 minutes before help arrives. Turning to his trapped friend he shares, "They say it's going to be 30 minutes before help gets here. On a night like tonight, I figure it will take longer. Sorry, looks like we're going to be later than I had first thought. Have you ever broken down before?" The two share adventure stories while waiting.

Meanwhile, remember, at the home of the wrecker guy who will help our pair, the wrecker guy's son is experiencing an asthma attack brought on by the weather change. His wife is overwhelmed with the situation. Our poor hero is caught between a cell phone flat tire rescue call, a decompensating wife and a child he's trying to keep from having a third trip to the ER this year.

Having calmed both the asthma attack and his wife, the exhausted man arrives to help the future concert attendees. It has been 45 minutes since the driver placed the call. The driver judges, "Forty-five minutes; it could have been worse." Then he rolls down his window and speaks to his pit crew.

"Sorry you're having to come out on a night like tonight. Looks like you're having an unexpected night like we are!"

"If you only knew," the broken and tired man replies.

"Really? What's up?"

"Kid so sick I may have to take him to ER again after I get done with you. My wife's freaking out. His hard breathing always messes with her."

"That's hard. Hey, can I pray for y'all?"

"Sure."

"What are your names?"

"I'm Joe. Wife is Sue. The boy is Ben."

"Father, heal Ben. Give Sue peace. Grant Joe wisdom and strength. Amen. I hate all this happening to ya. I'm gonna shut up and get out of your way. Kinda getting wet hanging out of my window!" (I wonder if NASCAR has seen as quick a tire change job as Joe is about to perform?) And, all the while, the passenger is watching, listening and pondering.

Our driver then turns his attention back to his friend. "We're going to be really late. Do you still want to go?"

"Not really. I've sat here, and watched and listened, and tried to process what you have. It's so foreign to me. However, it's what I long for. I want to have the peace you have. How'd you get there?"

The passenger's reply shouldn't startle us. That kind of reply should be the hope of our lives. Most of us would say that this made up story is too unrealistic. Really? Really? It seems to be the response that we find to Jesus' life and presence. He said what He did, we can also do.

Hard introspective question time: Would anybody want the Christianity you demonstrate in those times of the overwhelmingly unexpected hard events of life? Yeah, this one hurts me, too!

The Eagle Will Land

Some day our stormy journey will end. The ups and downs of life will lead us to a landing place. God will declare that His children's lives have been lived "good and faithful." I encourage you to join me in trying to live out my days here in agreement with Him, no matter the overwhelmingly unexpected.

About the Author

Dr. Doug Moore is a Family Practice physician. He has practiced medicine in Shelby County, Alabama since 1989. He has been married to Lisa since 1988. They have three children, three children-in-laws, one granddaughter, and three grand dogs.

He graduated from UAB School of Medicine in 1986 and completed his Family Practice Residency in Huntsville, AL, three years later. From there, he set up practice with his best friend from medical school. They have been at the same location since 1990.

He was raised in Southern Baptist churches. His first college he attended was a Catholic College. His undergraduate studies were completed at a Methodist college. He raised his children in a Presbyterian church. Currently he is a member of Church of the Highlands in Birmingham, Alabama. *More Than You Can Handle* is his attempt to put in print lessons learned in almost three decades of addressing the issues of life found in work, home, church and the rest of the world.

For more insight and inspiration, visit:
MoreThanYouCanHandle.com